THAILAND

INSIGHT *POCKET* GUIDES

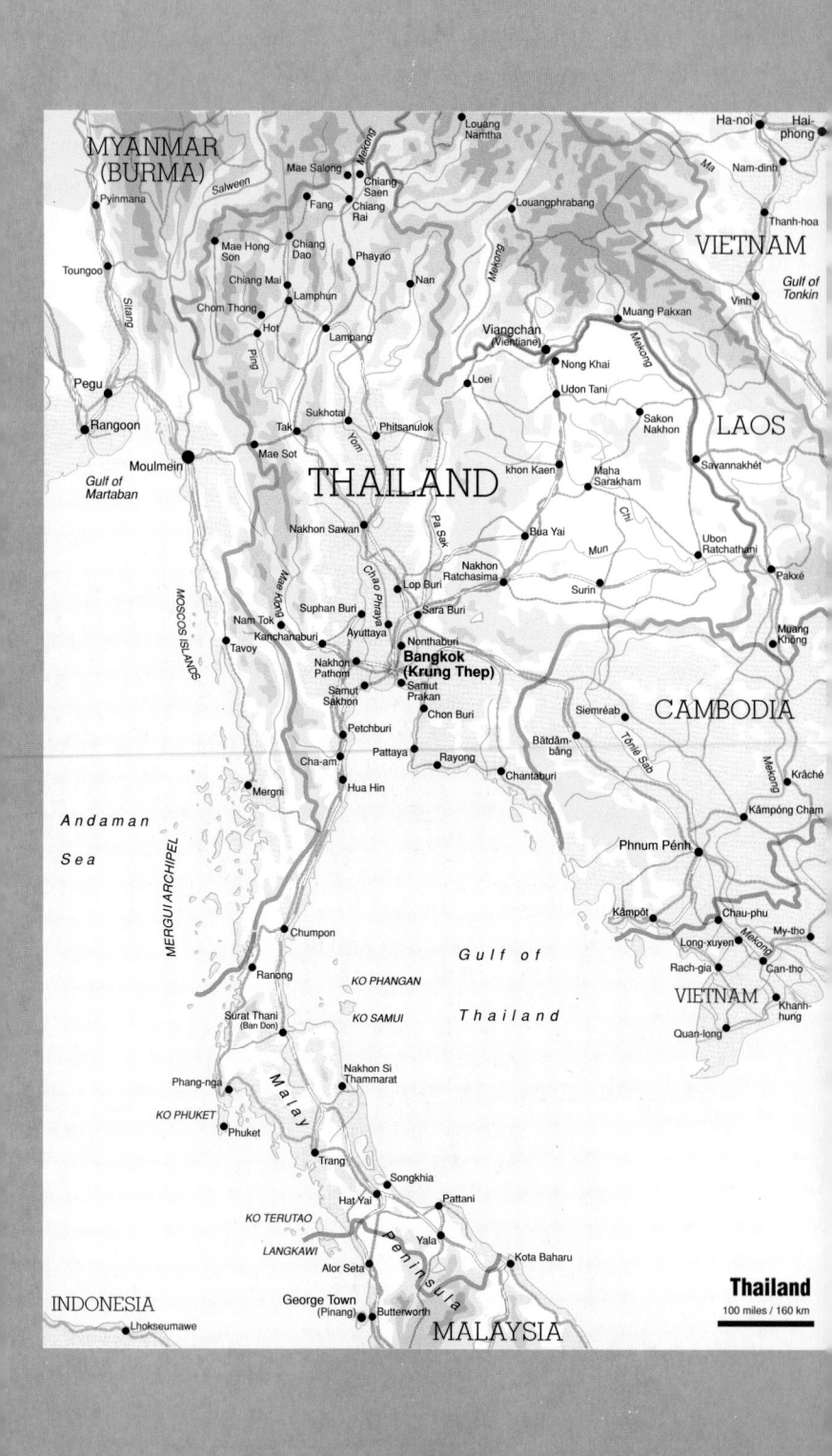

Dear Visitor!

For centuries, Thailand's magnetic appeal has turned short-term travellers into habitual visitors. What is the lure behind this fabled kingdom? For one thing, it is Thailand's cultural diversity, with its multitude of ethnic influences and a rich art and architecture that spans centuries. It is also a country in transition, filled with a dynamism that has transformed the landscape and made Thailand one of the success stories of Asia. But most of all, it is the people. The Thais are a gentle people, gracious and tolerant of outsiders' foibles.

Steve Van Beek, award-winning writer and our correspondent, came to Bangkok in 1969 for a short holiday. But, like many who came before him, Van Beek was so intrigued by the country and its people that he stayed on. 'The more I discovered of the country, the more enthralled I became. I was hooked for life,' says Van Beek, as if speaking of an old girlfriend instead of an adopted homeland.

Using Bangkok, Chiang Mai and the Northeast, and the southern resort isle of Phuket as hubs, Van Beek will launch you on your exploration of Thailand. Pick from his selection of full-day introductory tours, half- and full-day options and overnight excursions. And you will come across sights as diverse as boisterous street markets, fabled ancient cities, unspoilt hilltribe villages, verdant jungles and sparkling turquoise seas.

Be captivated by the charm of the Thai people; be entranced by its rich history and tradition and, like Van Beek, you will be most reluctant to leave this fascinating country.

Hans Höfer
Publisher, Insight Guides

C O N T E N T S

Pages 2/3:
Worshippers at the Temple
of Emerald Buddha

Pages 8/9:
Impish Thai school kids

Although bordering the ancient civilizations of China and India, Thailand is a relatively new country. Superbly-crafted Bronze Age implements and pottery found in the Northeastern town of Ban Chieng suggest that a sophisticated culture flourished there, perhaps as early as 3,500BC. Details of its history, however, are vague. In the 6th to the 8th century, Buddhist communities comprising Mon peoples from southern Burma were established west of present-day Bangkok at Nakhon Prathom (site of the world's tallest stupa) and 180km (112 miles) north at Lopburi. Both sites drew pilgrims from as far away as Sri Lanka.

Thailand's history as a nation began in the far north. Scholars are still debating whether proto-Thais drifted north through the mountains to settle in southern China (the Tai today comprise the largest ethnic minority in China), or arose in southern China and moved south into Thailand under the pressure of a growing population or of the Mongol hordes of Genghis Khan.

Whatever the explanation, by the 13th century, the Thais were well established in Chiengsaen on the Mekong River, and in Chiang Rai on the Kok River, a Mekong tributary. In the latter half of the 13th century, King Mengrai of Chiang Rai moved into the valley of the Ping River to establish a new capital at Chiang Mai in 1296.

Meanwhile, other Thai groups had filtered south through the mountains to the head of the Chao Phya River valley. They took over the Khmer city of Sukhothai and in 1238, King Intaradit formed a confederation of cities which eventually became the nation of Thailand, or Siam as it was then known.

Its greatest king, Ramkamhaeng, was an ally of Mengrai and with peace established between them, both kingdoms flourished in the fertile valleys. It was under Ramkamhaeng that a written language was formulated and many of the monuments of Sukhothai were erected. It also carried on the tradition of Buddhist scholarship established in Lopburi.

The Kingdom of Ayutthaya

A preoccupation with religion led to the city-state's decline as a political power and in 1351 a new kingdom to the south, Ayutthaya, assumed leadership. Ayutthayan kings were empire builders and the territory they ruled encompassed half of present-day Cambodia, most of Laos, the southern Burmese peninsula, and the four northern states of Malaysia.

Ayutthaya become a major regional trading power and its wealth attracted merchants from England, Portugal, Holland and France who set up trading posts there. The 17th century saw the rise of a Greek adventurer to virtual head of state, a situation which alarmed the Thais. In 1688, the Europeans were expelled and were not allowed to return until the early 19th century.

Throughout its history, Ayutthaya was engaged in wars with Cambodia and Burma. In 1767, fabled Ayutthaya, for 400 years one of the richest cities in the Orient, was overrun and torched by Burmese armies. Remnants of the Thai armies moved south to establish a new capital at Thonburi, a small village of Bangkok which had served as a customs port for Ayutthayan kings.

Burmese and Thais battling for Ayutthaya

Mural from Wat Phumin

Bangkok's Rise

In 1782, the new king, Chakri, established Bangkok as his capital city. He asked riverside Chinese merchants to move south-east to the Sampeng area which subsequently became the city's chief mercantile centre. On the land they vacated, he began construction of Wat Phra Kaew – the Temple of the Emerald Buddha – to hold the kingdom's most famous Buddha image.

War captives were employed to dig defensive moats in concentric arcs to the east of the original Klong (canal) Lawd. Rama I, the dynastic name he chose for himself, strove not only to establish a capital but to create a new Ayutthaya with symbols evoking its past grandeur and glory. The royal name for the city included the appellation Krung Thep, 'City of Angels' by which Ayutthaya had been known and the name modern Thais use for Bangkok.

Closed to foreigners for 150 years, Thailand began to open its doors to the outside world. By the 1830s, missionaries and a few merchants were living and working in the city and by 1860, trade and amity treaties had been established with North America and many countries of Europe.

The two kings credited with modernizing Thailand were King Mongkut (1851–68) and his son King Chulalongkorn (1868–1910). Mongkut, a remarkable man unfortunately lampooned in the movie *The King and I* (and still banned in Thailand), built the city's first paved street, New Road, in 1863. King Chulalongkorn continued the modernization process, building a rail line north, adding more city roads, constructing a tram line, and erecting most of the colonial-style public buildings in the capital.

As Bangkok moved into the 20th century, it began growing eastwards and northwards. Silom Road changed from a rural area of cattle markets, rice fields and market gardens into a residential neighbourhood. In 1932, the Memorial Bridge, the city's first, was built to link Bangkok and Thonburi and spurred development on the western side of the river. By the 1950s, most of the canals had been filled in and citizens no longer travelled on keels but on wheels.

The city's big construction boom came in the 1960s during the Vietnam War when vast amounts of money poured into Thailand.

King Chulalongkorn

The two-lane road that led to the rural Don Muang Airport was widened to four lanes and then, in the 1970s, to 10 lanes. With modernization came many of the traffic and communications problems that plague the city today. The 1980s saw the city alter direction from horizontal to vertical, with the skyline changing almost weekly. The economic boom of the late 1980s and early 1990s changed the city forever.

From a few dozen people, the city has burgeoned to nearly eight million souls. Aside from Chinatown, which has retained much of its cultural identity, most of the ethnic sections of the city have become homogenized.The markets and villagers have disappeared under shopping malls and Bangkok has come to resemble modern cities everywhere in the world.

Chiang Mai

Lanna, 'Land of a Million Rice Fields', is the name by which the North and its culture are known. Until the early part of this century, it existed as a separate kingdom with its own royal houses, dialect, and culture. Chiang Mai's history begins with King Mengrai who marched south from Chiengsaen to establish the city of Chiang Rai in 1262. After capturing Haripunchai (Lamphun) and securing joint leadership of Phayao, he sought a more central site in the Ping River Valley and established Chiang Mai (New City) in 1296.

The flowering of Lanna culture dates from the reign of warrior king Tilokaraja. He was so influential that the Eighth World Buddhist Council was held in Chiang Mai in 1455. A century later, a gigantic earthquake destroyed parts of the city including the upper portion of the great stupa of Wat Chedi Luang.

To add to its woes, Chiang Mai fell to the Burmese King of Pegu in 1558 and was ruled by Burma for the next two centuries. The

Kawila triumphed over the Burmese

hardships became so severe that, like several other cities of the North including Chiang Rai, Chiengsaen, Sukhothai and Phayao, the city's inhabitants simply abandoned it. It remained empty for 20 years until a Chiang Mai hero, Prince Kawila, re-populated it in 1796 and then triumphed over the Burmese in 1799.

A railway, begun in 1898 and completed in 1921, enabled the North to develop trade and communication links with Bangkok. In 1939, Chiang Mai was upgraded to a province and brought under the aegis of the Bangkok administration.

Phuket

History first takes note of Phuket in the *Kedah Annals of Malaysia* written around AD1200. The island was shared from an early date by Mon-Khmers from Burma who occupied the northern region and the Chao Lay (Sea Gypsies) who built settlements along the southern coast in the areas Rawai and Siray. Phuket, or 'Junkseilon' (a corruption of the Malay word 'Ujang Salang') as it appeared on

crude maps of the period, had an unsavoury reputation among 17th-century European sea captains. Captains' logs complained of pirates who preyed upon their ships along its shores, but by the 18th century, European ships were calling regularly to load up with fresh water, firewood, and pitch to caulk their boats. Later, merchants traded European products for ivory, gems and pearls.

In 1785, following the death of the island's governor, the Burmese attacked from the sea. Realising they were outnumbered, the governor's widow, Chan, and her sister, Mook, clothed the town's women in soldiers' uniforms. The great number of soldiers on the city's walls confused the Burmese and the Thais'

Phuket heroines, Mook and Chan swift, harassing sorties on their flanks weakened them. After a month, the Burmese decamped and sailed away. For their bravery, King Rama I conferred royal titles on the two women; a statue on the highway to town honours them.

When tin was discovered in the 1840s, Phuket town became the capital and within a few decades dominated the island's political and economic life. By the 1900s, rubber plantations blanketed the island's low hills. Today, tourism has nudged these two commodities aside as an important money-earner, although traces of their former importance can still be found in the rural areas and the back streets of Phuket's towns.

The People

Whether the original inhabitants were indigenous peoples or had migrated from China or Burma, their ethnic blood has been richly augmented by infusions of Vietnamese, Cambodian, Lao, Mon Burmese, Malay, Indian and even Persian strains to create a race recognisable as Thai. The most prominent minority group is the Chinese who, while retaining much of the culture of the Middle Kingdom, have been absorbed into the

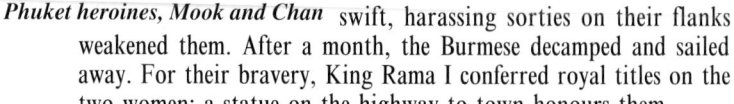

Craggy features of a Northern Thai

Thai fabric, making Thailand
rare among Asian countries in
having avoided class, ethnic, religious, or civil wars.

Northern and Northeastern
Thais and culture betray Lao
strains while the South has been
richly endowed by its proximity
to the Muslim culture of Malaysia. Both the North and the South
hold tribal peoples of surprising
diversity.

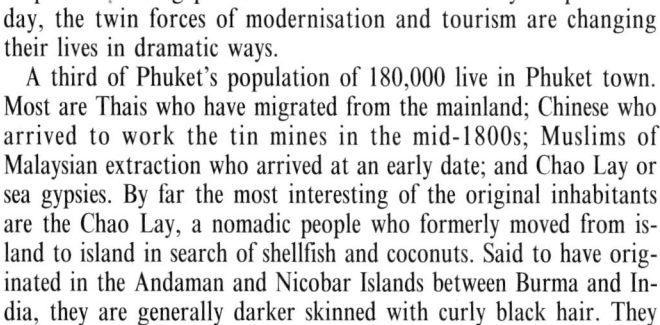

For most visitors, the animistic
hilltribes are the North's most
colourful inhabitants. Each of
the six principal groupings –
Hmong (Meo), Lisu, Akha, Lahu
(Musur), Mien (Yao) and Karen
– have distinct languages incom-
prehensible to the others. With ancient origins in China, they arrived in Thailand's northern hills in the past century. Despite their
cultural differences, there is little conflict between them.

Until recently, the hilltribes were nomadic farmers who practised
shifting cultivation. Many tribes also grew opium. To help improve
their lives, the Royal Family in the 1970s introduced new cash
crops and farming practices which the tribes readily adopted. Today, the twin forces of modernisation and tourism are changing
their lives in dramatic ways.

A third of Phuket's population of 180,000 live in Phuket town.
Most are Thais who have migrated from the mainland; Chinese who
arrived to work the tin mines in the mid-1800s; Muslims of
Malaysian extraction who arrived at an early date; and Chao Lay or
sea gypsies. By far the most interesting of the original inhabitants
are the Chao Lay, a nomadic people who formerly moved from island to island in search of shellfish and coconuts. Said to have orig-
inated in the Andaman and Nicobar Islands between Burma and India, they are generally darker skinned with curly black hair. They
speak their own language and follow their own animistic religion.

Thai Culture

Everything that one associates with the exotic Orient – fabulous
palaces, glittering temples, beautiful Buddha images, ornate art – is
found in abundance in Thailand. The Thais have a delicate touch
which transforms ordinary objects into works of art, a skill they
have applied to a wide range of practical and art objects.

Thai art has many antecedents but its artists have created a style
which is unique. Nothing can compare in design or execution with
the Temple of the Emerald Buddha and the Grand Palace. The
country has also produced a wide range of applied arts, most of

them for the purpose of beautifying temples. Mother-of-pearl was developed to decorate temple doors and royal utensils. Black and gold lacquer scenes often cover temple doors and windows. Murals on the inner walls of the temples tell the story of Buddha's life or

of his last incarnations before he was born as the Buddha. Buddha images have been carved from stone and wood, cast from bronze and shaped from clay, in a variety of styles and attitudes.

Dance and drama has been the principal mode of transmitting ancient stories. The most important source for theatrical productions has been the *Ramakhien*. This Thai version of the Indian classical tale, the *Ramayana*, tells the story of the abduction of the beauteous Sita, wife of the god-king Phra Ram, by the treacherous demon king Tosakan. The story is often depicted by huge leather shadow puppets, actors, masked actors, and puppets.

Chiang Mai is considered the cultural capital of Thailand. Its temples or *wats* are among the most beautiful in Asia.

A gilded Buddha image

While the Lanna or Northern style has been heavily influenced by Burmese architectural styles, its architects and artists have evolved a style distinct from its antecedents and unique in Thailand.

The South has also created its own arts and drama. Southerners were not monument builders so there is little architecture of consequence to view. It is in the realm of theatre that they excelled. The culture has been flavoured by contacts with Malaysia to produce a number of art forms distinctly different from those of Thailand's other regions. During a stay in Phuket, you may view one of the two most famous Southern creations, the *Nora* and the *Nang Talung*. The former is a dance-drama telling the story of a bird-goddess who falls in love with an earthling while the latter is shadow puppet theatre performed against a backlit cloth screen.

Thai Values

The Buddhist ideal of avoiding suffering has led to the adoption of an attitude of 'mai pen rai', translated variously as 'it doesn't matter' or 'no problem', and often accompanied by a shrug of the shoulders. The surprise is that despite this attitude, the Thais are a dynamic people as the rapid development of Bangkok attests.

Women enjoy a level of freedom not found in many countries. While many women in the lower economic groups have not yet obtained the protection from exploitation guaranteed by the constitution, those in the upper echelons have gained a degree of power envied by their sisters elsewhere. It is not unusual to see a major company helmed by a Thai woman.

Historical Highlights

3,500BC: Bronze Age culture created by an unknown people thrives at Ban Chieng located in Thailand's Northeast.

8th–12th century: Thais gradually migrate from China into northern Thailand which is controlled by the Khmer empire administered from Cambodia.

1238: Khmer power wanes and Thais led by King Intaradit, establish an independent nation based at Sukhothai.

1351: A new power at Ayutthaya, farther south on the Chao Phya River, supplants Sukhothai.

1767: After repeated attempts, Burmese armies succeed in overrunning Ayutthaya, stripping it of its population and treasures and putting it to the torch. The Thai army regroups at Thonburi and engages in 15 years of wars with the Burmese, Laotians and Vietnamese.

1782: The wars subside. General Chakri assumes the throne. Taking the name of Rama I, he establishes the Chakri dynasty of which the present king is the ninth monarch. Rama I moves his capital across the river to Bangkok.

1851–68: King Mongkut, the monarch depicted in *The King and I*, ascends the throne after 27 years as a Buddhist monk. He reforms the laws and sets Thailand on the path towards modernization. He encourages contact with the West, signing a far-reaching Treaty of Amity with the British in 1855.

1868–1910: King Chulalongkorn, one of history's most dynamic kings, continues his father's initiatives and Thailand moves firmly into the 20th century. By political maneuvering, he preserves Thailand's sovereignty, the only Southeast Asian nation that escapes colonization.

1911–25: King Vajiravudh concentrates on political reforms, giving greater freedom and encouraging criticism of government policies. Thailand sides with the Allies during World War I.

1925–35: Economic troubles stemming from the world economic depression compound King Pradajipok's problems and in 1932, a revolution occurs which replaces absolute monarchy with a constitutional monarchy.

1935–46: A young prince, Ananda Mahidol, is named king but he returns to Switzerland to complete his studies. Thailand is occupied by the Japanese during the war. In 1946, King Ananda dies and his younger brother, Bhumibol Adulyadej, is named king.

1950–73: On 5 May, Prince Bhumibol is crowned king. This is a time of turmoil for Thailand with numerous coups d'etat and a succession of military-backed governments. In the 1960s, Thailand experiences an economic boom as a result of investment by the US in support of the war effort in Vietnam. Tens of thousands of US soldiers are stationed in air bases scattered around the Northeast.

1973–90: A popular uprising topples a despised dictatorship, ushering in a period of true democracy. Various elements contrive to hamstring the democratic effort and create an atmosphere of strife and chaos. A violent right-wing counter-coup in 1976 reestablishes military rule. Several governments are chosen in popular elections but always with the military hovering in the background.

1991: Public reaction over a military coup d'etat against what it claims to be a corrupt government results in the appointment of former diplomat Anand Panyarachun as Prime Minister. His government is one of the most able and popular in 50 years.

1992: In May, public demand for a return to democracy leads to an army massacre that leaves hundreds dead. In September, elections are held and a new government under Chuan Leekpai is formed.

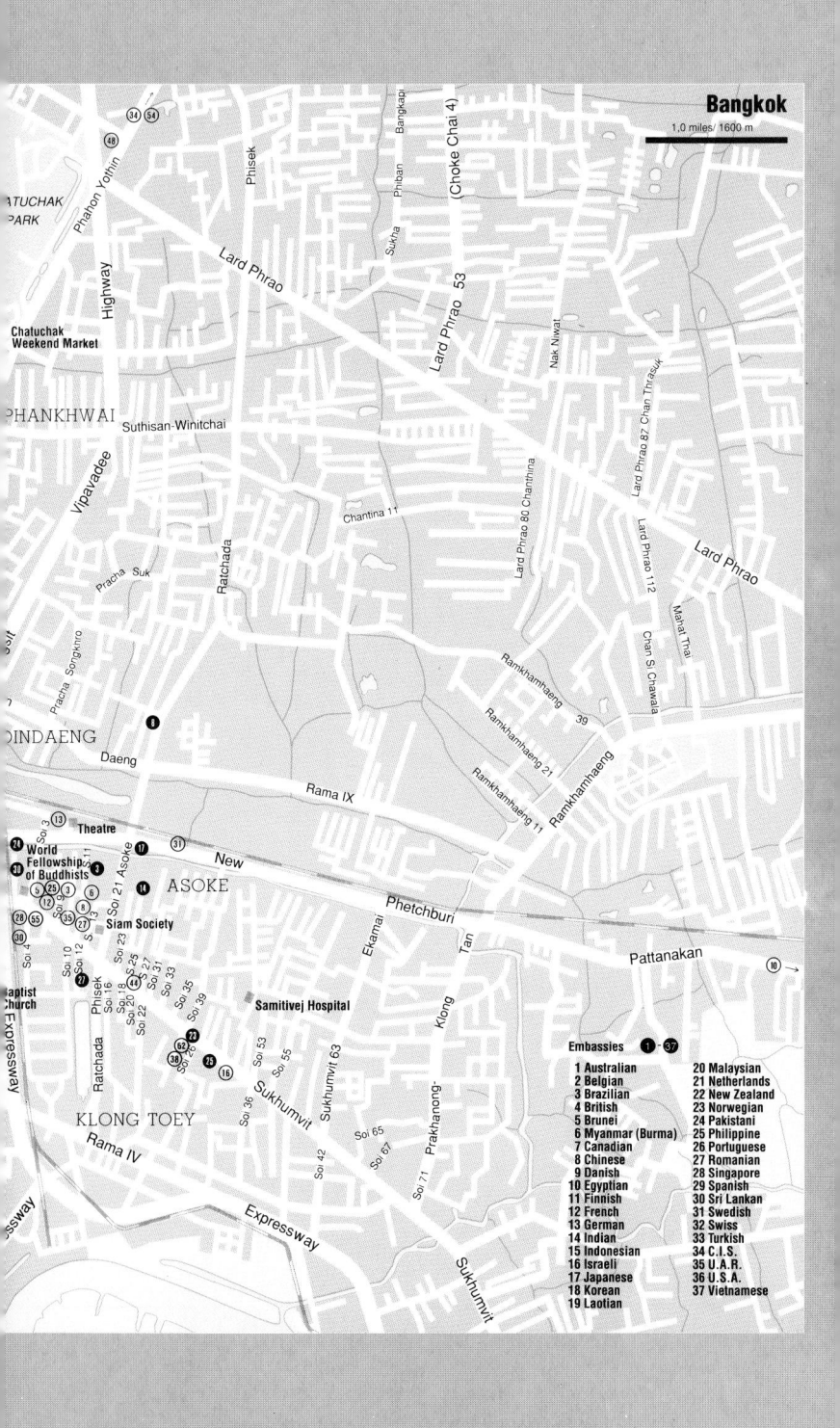

Bangkok

1,0 miles/ 1600 m

CHATUCHAK
PARK

Chatuchak
Weekend Market

PHANKHWAI

Chatuchak
Suthisan-Winitchai

Vipavadee

Phahon Yothin
Highway
Lard Phrao
Phisek
Bangkapi
(Choke Chai 4)
Phiban
Sukha
Lard Phrao 53
Nak Niwat
Lard Phrao 87 Chan Thrasuk
Lard Phrao 80 Chantina
Chantina 11
Lard Phrao 112
Lard Phrao

Pracha Suk
Ratchada
Mahat Thai
Chan S. Chawala

Pracha Songkhro
Ramkhamhaeng
Ramkhamhaeng 39

DINDAENG
Daeng
8
Ramkhamhaeng 21
Rama IX
Ramkhamhaeng 11
Ramkhamhaeng

13 Theatre
Soi 3
24 World
30 Fellowship
of Buddhists
Soi 21 Asoke
17
31
New
ASOKE
14
Phetchburi
Ekamai
Tan
Pattanakan
9 6 25 3 6
12 9
28 55 35 23 13
30 7 27
Siam Society
Soi 10
Soi 12
27
Soi 25 Soi 31
Soi 27
Soi 33
Soi 35
Soi 39
Samitivej Hospital
Klong
10

Phisek
Soi 16
44
Soi 20
Soi 22
Soi 53
Soi 55
Sukhumvit 63
Baptist
Church
Ratchada
Soi 36
62 22
38 29 16
Sukhumvit
Soi 65
Prakhanong
KLONG TOEY
Soi 42
Soi 67
Rama IV
Soi 71
Expressway
Expressway
Sukhumvit

Embassies   1 — 37

1 Australian
2 Belgian
3 Brazilian
4 British
5 Brunei
6 Myanmar (Burma)
7 Canadian
8 Chinese
9 Danish
10 Egyptian
11 Finnish
12 French
13 German
14 Indian
15 Indonesian
16 Israeli
17 Japanese
18 Korean
19 Laotian

20 Malaysian
21 Netherlands
22 New Zealand
23 Norwegian
24 Pakistani
25 Philippine
26 Portuguese
27 Romanian
28 Singapore
29 Spanish
30 Sri Lankan
31 Swedish
32 Swiss
33 Turkish
34 C.I.S.
35 U.A.R.
36 U.S.A.
37 Vietnamese

Bangkok

Bangkok is Thailand's capital city, whose dominance over the rest of the country is so absolute that it has the ability to shape the nation's perceptions and directions. Holding eight million people, it is 45 times larger than the second largest town, Chiang Mai, and is the national centre for administration, religion, and commerce.

Its higgledy-piggledy growth over the past few centuries presents a challenge for the visitor trying to find his way around. There is no grid system for the streets. A street can have four different names along its length; there is no distinct business or diplomatic districts; nor are there any easily identifiable landmarks. More often than not, shops, restaurants and houses do not display street numbers. Although few Thais are fluent in English, they are ever willing to help lost visitors. Stop a Thai to ask directions and, likely as not, he will personally walk you to your destination. The upside of the challenge is that there are numerous lanes and alleys into which one can wander to discover many of Bangkok's secrets. Other than a few purse snatchers and pickpockets, street crime directed against travellers is rare, even at night in darkened alleys.

Days 1 and 2 are designed to give you a flavour of the city. They are followed by several half-day itineraries which take you deeper into the city's heart. The itineraries cover only the daylight hours. See the *Eating Out* and *Nightlife* sections for evening activities.

Come fly with me

*Right:
Bangkok's
urban crawl*

Shrine, Market and Canals

Breakfast in Lumpini Park, followed by a visit to Erawan Shrine and Pratunam Market. Stop for lunch at Sky Lounge, and then embark on a boat-ride into the canals, ending the day at the Author's Lounge of the Oriental Hotel for tea. Casual wear but not sloppy. The Oriental has been known to turn away non-hotel guests for wearing sleeveless blouses, shorts or sandals.

Begin at 7am with a walk in a park that gives you an intimate peek into the ways Thais wake up in the morning. It will also provide a hint of the city's dynamism. **Lumpini Park** (named after the Nepalese town in which Buddha was born) wears two faces: in the morning, it is dominated by the Chinese; in the afternoon, the Thais. Sometime during your stay, plan a late afternoon visit.

As the sun rises, joggers pound Lumpini's pavements and workers hurry to work, grabbing bowls of noodles from sidewalk vendors. Health-conscious Chinese perform *tai chi chuan* exercises, and would-

Lumpini at dawn

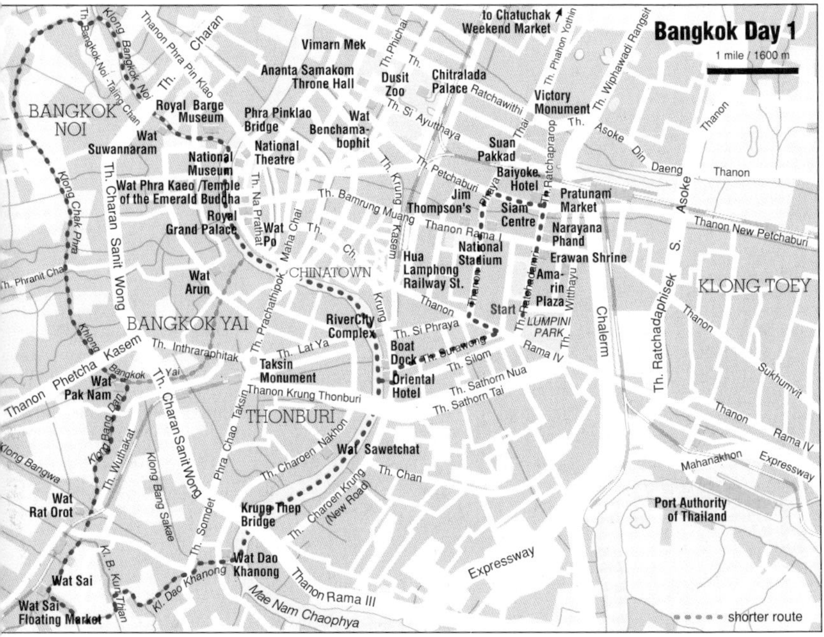

shorter route

be Chinese warriors mime ancient rituals with silver swords. On Sunday, rent a boat and paddle to the island where Chinese gather to play and sing ancient songs. For a ringside seat of the passing scene, head for the north-west corner of the park to **Pop** restaurant for an American or Thai breakfast under the trees.

After breakfast, exit the western gate onto Rajdamri Road. Plan your departure so that you arrive at **Narayana Phand** at opening hours at 10am. It is a 1-km (½-mile) journey north (to the right) along Rajdamri to Rajprasong. If it is not cool enough to walk, cross the street and catch a bus (any route number will do), taxi or *tuk tuk*. Get off just before the busy Rajprasong (Raatprasong) intersection, the first four-way intersection you encounter.

Cross to the **Erawan Shrine** on the corner, an oasis of peace

Erawan Shrine

away from the din and bustle of the 20th century. The Brahma image is famed for granting wishes for success in love, examinations and the lottery. Start your Bangkok vacation on a good note by buying incense, candles and flowers and uttering a short prayer for good luck. If you're lucky you may see Thai dancers moving gracefully to traditional music.

From the Erawan Shrine, head north along Rajdamri to the shopping mall (127 Rajdamri Road) with the giant *yaksa* standing guard before its doors. This is Narayana Phand, the government's handicraft store. The quality of the goods is mediocre but the range is extensive; a short browse gives a good idea of the variety of crafts that Thailand produces.

Pratunam market vendor

Next, explore a real market called **Pratunam**. To get there, exit Narayana Phand, turn right, cross the canal and at the intersection walk across Petchburi Road under the overpass, where Rajdamri changes its name to Rajaparop Road.

Begin by looking at the displays of the sidewalk vendors. When you see a lane running to the right between the buildings, follow it and plunge into the wet market which lies behind the building facades. From here on, forget directions and just wander among the stalls that sell fresh produce and practical items that Thais use in their daily lives. A walk represents a trip into the heart of Thai city life as it was before supermarkets were invented, and it is a must for people-watchers. Sit down for a soft drink at one of the open-fronted restaurants and watch all the activities.

Back on Rajaparop, head 250m (820ft) north to the pedestrian bridge and cross to the Indra Hotel. Just behind the hotel is Bangkok's tallest building, **Baiyoke Suite Hotel** (130 Rajprarop Road. Tel: 255-0330/41), painted in rainbow colours.

Ride the elevator to **Sky Lounge** restaurant on the 43rd floor of the hotel. Enjoy its magnificent panoramic view of the city and lunch on Thai, Chinese, or European food. Use your map to orient yourself on the city's landmarks.

After lunch, walk back to a point opposite the entrance of the Indra Hotel, where an opening leads to a maze of lanes. Also considered part of Pratunam Market, this section is devoted to clothing, tailors and sundries. Browse and then exit the market and catch a taxi to the **Oriental Hotel** (48 Oriental Avenue, New Road, Tel: 236-0400, 236-0420).

The morning has probably been hot, hard work, so spend the afternoon relaxing on a cool boat ride through the canals. Walk up the driveway to the Oriental but, instead of entering, continue past the entrance doors and down a ramp to the right. It leads to a lane that runs between the northern wall of the hotel and the southern wall of the adjacent French Embassy. At the end of the lane is a small boat dock where you can hire a boat. You want a motor launch (*rua yone*) not the long-tailed boats. These smaller boats are quieter and hold 8–10 people comfortably. The price will depend on your bargaining ability but should be around 350 baht an hour. Tell them you will need it for about three hours.

Over the past few decades, most of Bangkok's canals have been transformed into streets. To see how Thais once lived, head into the canals on the Thonburi side. Ask the boatman to travel upriver to **Klong** (canal) **Bangkok Noi**. This route will take you past **Wat Arun** (The Temple of Dawn), the tall spire on your left; **Wat Po**, shortly after it on the right; and the gleaming **Emerald Buddha/Grand Palace** complex, also on your right.

Shortly before reaching the Phra Pinklao Bridge, the boatman will turn left into Klong Bangkok Noi. Three hundred metres (984ft) in on the right, ask the boatman to stop at the **Royal Barge Museum.** Kept here are the most important barges in the Royal Fleet of 51 which undertake grand river processions on special occasions; the last occurred in 1987 on King Bhumibol's 60th birthday. The 44-metre (144-ft) long vessel with the graceful, swan-head prow is the **Sri Suphannahongse** in which the Royal Family rides. A video captures the stirring procession in all its brilliance.

Continue up Bangkok Noi until you reach **Klong Chak Phra** where you turn left. Among the palm trees are many beautiful old houses. Klong Chak Phra changes its name to Klong Bang Kounsri and then Klong Bangkok Yai. If you have seen enough by this point, continue along Bangkok Yai until you re-enter the river

The haunting Wat Arun (Temple of Dawn) is ironically best seen at dusk

with Wat Arun on your left. Return to the Oriental. This portion of the journey should take about two hours.

If you are keen for further adventure, turn right from Klong Bangkok Yai into Klong Ban Dan. The corner is marked by a shop selling ornate coffins. You then pass **Wat Sai**, site of the former Floating Market. Continue into Klong Sanam Chai and the jungled area known as Suan Phak (vegetable garden). From here, continue into Klong Dao Khanong and enter the river below the Krung Thep Bridge.

It is a long but pleasant ride upriver past warehouses, riverside homes, and shipyards where wooden fishing trawlers are repaired. In the late afternoon sun, the scene glows in the warm light and acquires a magical aura. Disembark at the **Oriental Hotel**.

The Oriental is one of Asia's classic hotels and the **Author's Lounge** is one reason why. Order tea or freshly-brewed coffee and relax for a while under bamboo trees. If, instead, you feel like a late afternoon drink, sit on the terrace and watch the river go by. For dinner, take the free boat ride from the Oriental across the river to dine at the **Sala Rim Naam** restaurant. It offers a set Thai meal on the banks of the Chao Phya and a programme of classical dancing.

Tea at the Author's Lounge

If you are still feeling energetic, return to the Erawan Shrine (closes at 11pm) to see it in another mood. There, or up Ploenchit Road, buy a few fragrant *puang malai*. Laid on your bed, the beautiful floral garlands will perfume your room all night – a reminder of your first magical day in Thailand.

DAY 2

Temple of the Emerald Buddha and Grand Palace

Breakfast in a garden, then experience the grandeur of the Temple of the Emerald Buddha and the Grand Palace. Next, visit the Coins and Decoration Museum followed by a massage at Wat Po, cooling off with a swim at your hotel and dinner in a Thai house.

Begin the day with breakfast in a hotel garden. **The Regent Bangkok**, the **Hilton International**, and the **Siam Intercontinental** are three ideal choices. After breakfast, take a taxi to **Wat Phra**

Guardians of the Chapel Royal

Kaew, the **Temple of the Emerald Buddha**.

No other temple complex so typifies Thai art as this one does. Its glittering surfaces and wealth of art makes it one of Asia's architectural wonders. The 100-baht ticket admits you to Wat Phra Kaew, the Grand Palace, the Wat Phra Kaew Museum, the Coins and Decorations Museum and Vimarn Mek across town (keep your ticket if you plan to do Itinerary 1, *Pick & Mix*). The Wat Phra Kaew is the single most important Buddhist monument in Thailand. Its principal building, the **Chapel Royal**, was constructed in 1784 to house the kingdom's most sacred Buddha image. Sitting high on a pedestal, the jadeite image surprises many visitors by its small size. That it is venerated in such a lavish manner leaves no doubt about its importance to Thai Buddhists.

Among the other buildings guarded by the *yaksa* (giant demons) are the trio of structures to the right of the Chapel Royal. The one on the east is the **Prasad Phra Thepidon** or Royal Pantheon which holds the statues of the first eight kings of the Chakri dynasty, the current monarchical house. To the west, the **Library** holds the Tripataka, the holy Buddhist scriptures. The tallest structure is the huge gilded **Phra Si Ratana Chedi**, covered in gold mosaic tiles. Just north of these monuments is a model of **Angkor Wat**, the great holy city of the Khmer empire in the 11th and 12th centuries.

The walls of the cloisters around the complex are covered in murals recounting the *Ramakhien* story. Look in the outer areas of each scene for charming depictions of daily life and entertainments.

From Wat Phra Kaew, walk south into the compound where the **Grand Palace** is located. Since 1946, the Thai royal family has lived in Chitrlada Palace in the northern area of Bangkok, but the Grand Palace is still used for state ceremonies and for receiving foreign dignitaries.

The first building you reach is the **Amarin Vinitchai Throne** which served as royal residences for Ramas I, II and III. In the first hall is the boat-shaped throne where legal cases requiring royal adjudication were heard. Behind it was Rama I's bedchamber.

Main courtyard, Wat Phra Kaew

Since his reign, each new monarch has slept in it the first night after his coronation.

The centrepiece is the majestic **Chakri Maha Prasad** with its three spires atop an Italian Renaissance building. Constructed in 1882, it was the last building to be erected in the Grand Palace. Wander through the state drawing rooms which are decorated in the manner of European palaces with some very Thai touches to maintain the perspective.

To the west is the **Dusit Maha Prasad**, or Audience Hall where Kings once conducted state businesses. It is now the final resting place for deceased kings before they are cremated in the nearby Sanam Luang field. On the left of the complex is a lovely little restaurant with an open verandah. Here, you can enjoy lunch and a panoramic view of the Dusit Maha Prasad.

Afterwards, exit the Grand Palace, turn right, and walk past the ticket booth to the **Coins and Decoration Museum**. Here you will find ceramic coins, silver bullet money, seals and money from the other regions of Thailand and the world. Upstairs are beautiful royal crowns, jewelled swords, jewellery, brocaded robes, betelnut sets and royal decorations.

Stone statue, Wat Po

Exit the complex onto Na Prathat Road to the north. Turn left and walk along the wall towards the river. At the corner, turn left again and walk along the Grand Palace Wall. Pass the next intersection and turn left at the second corner. A short way down on the left is the entrance to **Wat Po**.

Restored many times, Wat Po is one of Bangkok's most eclectic *wats* and it is well worth spending a half hour sitting and watching its various activities. Of special interest is the 45-metre (148-ft) long, gilded **Reclining Buddha** in the north-west corner. Examine the soles of the feet which bear, in intricate mother-of-pearl patterns, the 108 signs by which a Buddha can be recognised. In the courtyard are statues of *rusi* (ascetics) demonstrating exercises to keep the body strong and limber (Wat Po has a famous herbal medicine school). Do not miss the *bot* (ordination hall) to the right of the entrance with its marvellous mother-of-pearl doors and its sandstone bas-relief panels depicting scenes from the *Ramakhien*, the classical saga of the god-king Rama. Pull the stone ball from the mouth of a Chinese stone lion without breaking the ball or the mouth and you are guaranteed eternal life.

On the eastern side of the courtyard is the **School of Traditional Massage**. You pay 120 baht for an hour-long massage that will soothe travel-weary muscles. Thai masseurs dig a little deeper than those of other disciplines but enduring it will result in a truly relaxed body by the end of the hour.

In the late afternoon, return to your hotel for a cool swim. In the evening, dine on Thai cuisine at **Lemongrass** in an old Thai house at 5/1 Soi 24, Sukhumvit Road. Tel: 258-8637.

Right: carved detail from the ornate roof of the Grand Palace

1. Marble Wat, Dusit Zoo and Teak Palace

To the Marble Wat to watch monks receive alms; the zoo to see exotic Asian animals; then on to Vimarn Mek, billed as 'the world's largest Golden Teak structure' with its lovely art collection (open Wednesday through Sunday).

Each morning before dawn, some 100,000 Buddhist monks throughout the kingdom don their saffron robes and walk barefooted through village and city streets. Buddhist families waiting outside their homes place rice and curries in the silent monks' black *baht* (alms bowls) which they will later eat at their monasteries.

The ritual is slightly altered at **Wat Benjamabophit** (the Marble Wat). Here, Thais take the food to the monks who wait in the tree-shaded street before the temple. It is a moving sight and offers a chance for some superb photos.

About 6.30am, ask a taxi driver to take you to Wat Benjamabophit. Watch the alms giving which continues until 7.30am. Take all the photos you like and then proceed through the gate into the temple courtyard.

Wat Benjamabophit was built in 1900, the last major temple constructed in Bangkok. Designed in cruciform shape, the exterior of the *viharn* (prayer hall) is clad in Italian carrara marble, hence it's name, the Marble Wat. Go inside. The stained glass windows depicting praying angels are a radical departure from tradition, both in the material used as well as in the treatment of the sub-

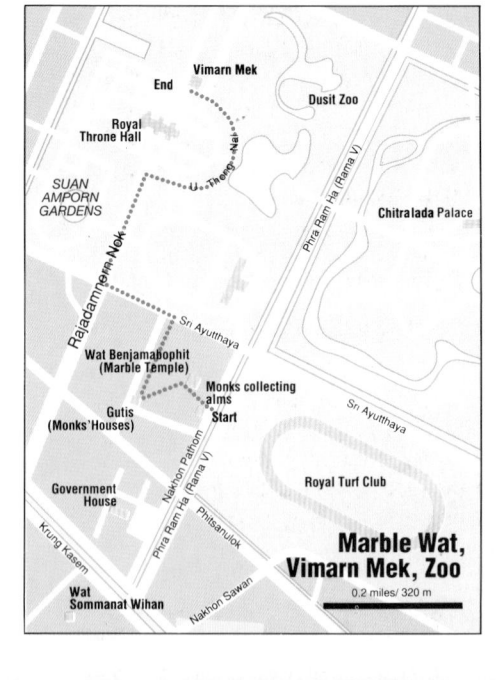

Marble Wat, Vimarn Mek, Zoo
0.2 miles/ 320 m

jects. The Buddha image is a superb copy of Phitsanuloke's famed Phra Buddha Jinnarat which is said to have wept tears of blood when Ayutthaya overran the northern town in the 14th century.

In the cloisters behind the *bot*, King Chulalongkorn placed copies of important Asian **Buddha images** to show his subjects the many ways in which the Buddha had been portrayed in Asia throughout history. Exit the *wat* through the northern door onto Sri Ayutthaya Road. Walk left to the next intersection. Turn right into the broad plaza with its equestrian statue of King Chulalongkorn. Walk past it to the **Ananta Samakom Throne Hall**, the former home of Parliament; unfortunately, it is not open to the public. Walk around it to the right.

Halfway around on the right is the gate to **Dusit Zoo** (Khao Din). This is Bangkok's only zoo and it provides a good introduction to the animals of Asia's jungles. The rhinos, the large aviary, the orang utan, and the royal white elephants are special favourites.

About 10am, return to the zoo entrance and continue the same direction you were going before. Behind the Throne Hall is a gate marked 'Vimarn Mek'. At the doorway, present the ticket you bought at the Grand Palace (Day 2) or pay the 50-baht entrance fee. Free 45-minute guided English-language tours are conducted at half-hour intervals beginning at 9.45am (last tour at 2.45pm). You are not allowed to wander on your own.

Receiving alms at the Marble Wat

Vimarn Mek (Celestial Residence) was built by King Chulalongkorn as an informal alternative to the stately Grand Palace. The 81-room house and the gardens alone would merit a visit, but it is the art collection that makes it especially interesting.

From here, you can head uptown for lunch or return to the zoo for a Thai-style lunch at one of its many restaurants. Go local and try a *Guay Tiew Phat Thai*, a tasty noodle dish.

2. Chinatown

A walk through Chinatown, a visit to a Chinese Buddhist temple and a trip to a market straight out of ancient China.

You can get up a bit later to start this one. The route takes you straight north through the heart of Chinatown. Ride a boat or taxi to the **Tha Rachawong** landing on Rachawong Road. Walk 50m (164ft) to Songwat Road on the right. The corner is marked by a beautiful gray and green trading firm whose architecture seems a blend of Moorish and German.

Turn right into Songwat Road which parallels the waterfront. Songwat feels different from other city streets, exuding the air of old-time mercantile trading. Walk 200m (656ft) to the tree-shaded Chinese temple, **Sanjao Kao** (Old Shrine), on the left. The lane just before it is marked **Soi Itsaranuphap** (also spelled 'Issaranuphap' and on some signs, Soi 16, Charoenkrung); you will be walking it all the way to its end, a distance of 1km (½ mile).

Pass through the doors guarded by giant scowling sentinels. Hanging from the ceiling are incense coils spiralling scented blue smoke to the heavens. The altar before Kuan Im (Goddess of Mercy) and other guardian gods is generally filled with offerings of fruit and brightly-coloured cakes. Plaques and photographs honour dead souls.

Just beyond the *sanjao* is a beautiful old school in colonial style architecture. You then pass spice shops with sticks of cinnamon and other herbs; you will know them by their heady fragrances. Near the end of the lane, on the right, is a shop making Chinese lanterns; watch the artists at work and then buy a pair of lanterns for about 300 baht.

Chinese temple mural

From here on, directions are provided but you are free to make your own discoveries. Cross Soi Wanit I. Forty metres (131ft) down the road, on the right, at 369/1 is the lovely **Sanjao Guan Oo**; step inside for a few moments and absorb its atmosphere. Con-

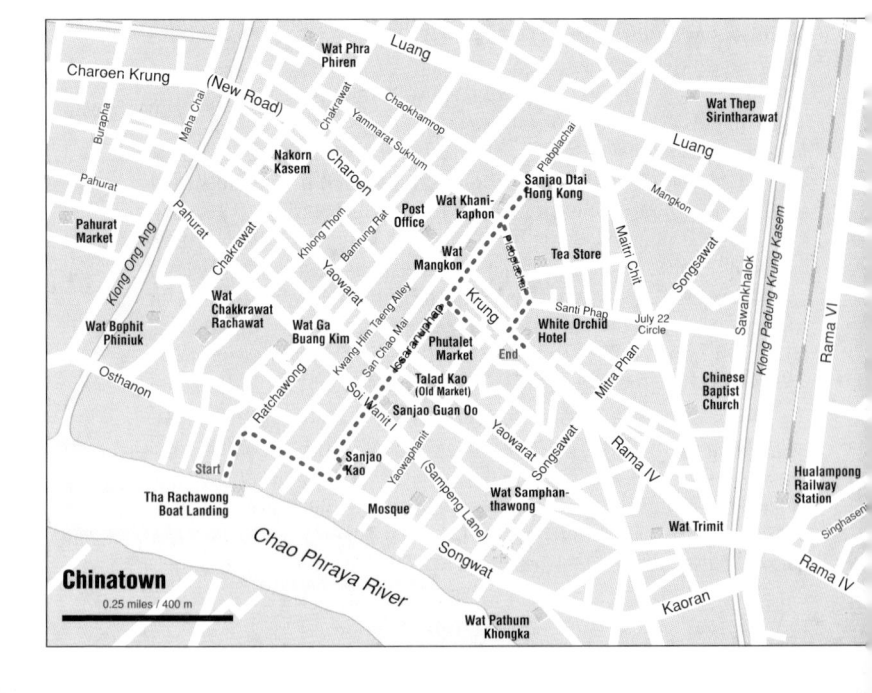

Chinese banner painter

tinue down the *soi* past the shops selling shrimp crackers and fried fish maw. Pass the entrance to Talad Kao (Old Market) to arrive at one of Chinatown's arteries: Yaowarat Road.

Cross this road and buy a Chinese apple from one of the stalls. About 60m (197ft) further down Itsaranuphap, turn right into **Phutalet Market**, also known as Talad Mai (New Market). The market is a bit scruffy but rich with the scents of seafood, Chinese foodstuffs and pastries, and has a medieval European feel to it.

Retrace your steps to Soi Issaranuphap, turn right and continue north. Cross New Road (Charoen Krung) and enter a lane that, more than any other section of the city, breathes of old China. Here, you will find paper funeral clothes, temple banners, incense sticks 3m (10ft) tall, paper money, and dozens of other fascinating items. The *soi* ends at Plabplachai Road. On the corner are shops selling houses, Mercedes Benz, and even cellular telephones made of paper, an art form called *kong tek*. Chinese burn these *kong tek* items, sending them to the afterlife to serve deceased relatives.

Exit Soi Issaranuphap and walk straight ahead along **Plabplachai Road**. Just past Wat Kanikaphon on your left are doors bearing a pair of giant Chinese warriors who guard the Mahayana Buddhist **Sanjao Dtai Hong Kong**. Enter it. If you are lucky, Chinese worshippers will be burning *kong tek* items in a tall furnace. If not, watch the devotees lighting candles and paying obeisance in a manner unlike that of the Thais.

Return to the mouth of Soi Issaranuphap. Turn into Plabplachai which angles left towards New Road. Near the intersection is an astrologer's studio with a picturesque curtain covering its front door. Along this street are several stores selling Chinese tea in canisters inscribed with large characters. Savour the scents of ancient China and buy whatever blend appeals to you. Have lunch at a sidewalk noodle stall or continue to New Road, and turn left. A few metres down is the **White Orchid Hotel** (409–421 Yaowarat Road. Tel: 226-0026) which has a good air-conditioned Chinese restaurant on its mezzanine. From here, catch a taxi back to your hotel.

3. Suan Pakkad Palace and Jim Thompson House

A visit to an antique teak royal palace and a beautiful Thai-style home filled with beautiful objects.

Whimsically-named, **Suan Pakkad** (Cabbage Patch) **Palace** was the home of the Prince of Nagor Svarga and his wife Princess Chumbhot. The fine stout teak houses were transported from the north

Interior of Jim Thompson House

and erected around a pond stalked by pelicans. To get there, take a taxi to **No. 352 Sri Ayutthaya Road** (nearly opposite the Siam City Hotel) and wander through the complex. Pause to look at the fine Ayutthayan-period manuscript cabinets with their lacquer and gold decorations. Other rooms hold various superb examples of Thai classical art. The Princess was an avid collector of Ban Chieng pottery and neolithic artifacts and these are housed in the back building on the right.

Suan Pakkad's centrepiece is the **Lacquer Pavilion**, one of the finest examples of gold and black lacquer work in Asia and a priceless work of art. It has been reconstructed from two *ho trai* or monastic libraries. The interior walls are richly decorated with Buddhist scenes. Note the depiction of 17th-century European visitors wearing plumed hats and riding fat horses. Suan Pakkad (Tel: 245-4934) is open daily, except Sunday, from 9am–4pm; Admission: 80 baht (includes a free fan; very handy on a hot day).

When you've had enough of Suan Pakkad, take a taxi to the **Jim Thompson House**, located at the end of **Soi Kasemsan 2** on Rama I Road across from the National Stadium. Silk king Jim Thompson's life was as mysterious as was his disappearance two decades ago in Malaysia's Cameron Highlands while on a Sunday afternoon walk. Like Suan Pakkad, the Jim Thompson House is an assemblage of six Ayutthayan teak houses to create the archetypical Thai-style house. Thai houses are built-in panels attached to pillars by wooden pegs and so are eminently transportable. The house is stunning as is the peaceful garden setting and the art collection. Enjoy the calls of the tropical birds. There are also excellent reproductions of old maps and wall hangings for sale on the ground floor. Jim Thompson House (Tel: 215-0122) is open Monday–Saturday from 9am–4.30pm. The 100-baht ticket price includes a guided tour in English or French.

4. Nonthaburi

A ride up the river, lunch at a floating restaurant, a provincial market, the beautiful riverside Wat Chalerm Phra Kiet, and a fast boat home through the back canals.

Head up the Chao Phya River to experience river scenery, a lush plantation, and two rural temples. Catch an express boat (the long, low white ones with red trim) travelling to the right from the landings at The Oriental Hotel, Royal Orchid Sheraton, Grand Palace (Tha Chang Wang Luang), Thammasat University (Tha Prajan), or Thewes. Plan to leave around 11am so you can lunch in Nonthaburi. Ride for 45 minutes to the terminus at Nonthaburi. Along the way look out for houses on stilts, sawmills, and picturesque riverside temples.

Disembark at **Nonthaburi** and turn right along the promenade past the turn-of-the-century wooden provincial office and the lampposts bearing pungent-smelling *durian* fruits which Nonthaburi was once famous for. At the end of the seawall is **Rim Fang Floating Restaurant** where you can dine on Thai food while watching the river.

Return to the dock, explore the market and then catch a ferry across the river. After disembarking, walk straight about 70m (230ft), passing the open-fronted wooden shops on the right. Just before a new four-storey block of shophouses, turn right onto a sidewalk that skirts the shophouses and enter a sawmill where logs floated down from northern forests are cut into boards.

Cross the yard, and exit the doorway in the opposite wall onto a path set with paving stones. Roughly parallel to the river, this palm-shaded path runs a zigzag course through coconut plantations, orchid nurseries and a small village. Halfway along is Wat Salak Dtai; continue past it. If lost, ask for 'Wat Ja-lerm'.

Fifteen minutes from the pier, you arrive at what seems to be a fortress wall; beyond it is the riverside **Wat Chalerm Phra Kiet**, one of Bangkok's most beautiful *wats* as much for its architecture as for its setting. The tall *chedi* (stupa) stands behind a *bot* (ordination hall) that is flanked by two *viharn* (prayer halls). The buildings' gables are covered in Chinese ceramic tiles, a style in vogue during the reign of King Rama III (1824–51).

Wat Chalerm Phra Kiet

The Fine Arts Department has done a superb job of restoring the buildings. After admiring the fine paintings (ask a monk to

Up the canal in a long-tailed boat

open the doors), exit the gateway on the riverside and enter a compound of raintrees. Beyond the wall are three pavilions where you can enjoy a view of the river.

Retrace your steps to the ferry boat pier. Three bus lines run from here into the countryside; ask for the bus to **Bang Kluai** (Baang Kluay). The 20-minute scenic trip will take you past fields and houses and into the town of Bang Kluai, stopping opposite Wat Chalaw. Cross the street and walk through the *wat* gate (also signposted as the 'Bang Kluai Police Station') to see work in progress on one of the most ambitious architectural undertakings in Thailand. On the left, a *bot* is being built in the shape of a huge Sri Suphannahongse, the principal Royal Barge (mentioned in the *Day 1* Itinerary). At 95m (312ft) long, it is twice the length of the original vessel. It will take years to complete but the mirror mosaics already in place suggest that it is going to be a spectacular structure when finished. Also look at some of the superb Buddha images in the porticoes of nearby buildings.

To return home, walk to the canal at the far side of the *wat* compound. You can either hire a flat-bottomed speedboat which will zip you down the canal on a hair-raising trip (price must be bargained; usually 100 baht regardless of the number of passengers) or catch the regular long-tailed boat (6 baht). Both boats will head left down Klong Bangkok Noi to the Tha Chang boat landing next to the Grand Palace.

5. Chatuchak Weekend Market

Browse in one of the Orient's great bazaars with everything imaginable at bargain prices.

The sprawling **Chatuchak Weekend Market** on the northern end of the city is an open-air supermarket frequented by Thais and stocked with the most extraordinary items, including pet puppies. Well worth a browse even if you aren't in a buying mood. Open Saturday and Sunday, it is already humming by 6am. Take a taxi or Bus No. 29 or 34 up north along **Paholyothin Road** and disembark just before you reach the

Puppy love

Central Plaza Hotel and the intersection with the Vipavadee Rangsit Highway. Look for the long fence on the left with the vendor's stalls behind it.

Orient yourself according to the **clocktower** that stands high above the stalls in the centre of the sprawling complex. Then begin your exploration.

To the right you will find household items, fresh produce, clothing and, most interesting of all, a huge pet emporium with everything from exotic birds and fish to monitor lizards and other unusual animals. To the left are more cheap clothes, used books, Thai musical instruments, stamps, antiques, and art and craft items. Plant enthusiasts should cross **Yan Paholyothin Road** (runs along the southern edge of the complex) to the plant market which resembles a mini-jungle.

Clock tower at Chatuchak

Nancy Chandler's *Market Map* (from major bookstores) details the location of each item but it is equally fun just to wander aimlessly. Many visitors return here weekend after weekend, fascinated not only by the huge variety of goods but by the milling crowds (mainly Thais), the banter of bargaining, and the atmosphere of the East that envelopes them in a way few city markets can.

At noon, have lunch at the **Vegetarian Restaurant** operated by Bangkok's former mayor. The variety of vegetarian dishes is astounding and the prices are too cheap to believe. Find it at the south-western corner near the bus stop on Yan Paholyothin. The market closes at 6pm. The restaurant is open daily Tuesday through Sunday from 6am to 2pm.

Papier-mâché pigs aplenty

Excursions

6. By River to Ayutthaya

A cruise up the Chao Phya River to Ayutthaya, Thailand's majestic capital from 1351–1767. Buffet lunch/dinner served aboard ship.

For four centuries, **Ayutthaya**, 60km (37 miles) upriver from Bangkok, served as Thailand's capital. Its magnificent temples and palaces, and more than 2,000 gleaming golden spires impressed early European visitors who filled their journals with paeans to its glory. Destroyed in 1767 by Burmese invaders, even in ruins it evokes the majesty of one of Asia's great empires.

The way to approach it is as all European explorers of the 17th century did: via the **Chao Phya River.** Two river cruisers provide the opportunity. The sleek *Oriental Queen* departs the Oriental Hotel each morning at 8am, cruising upriver past the city's major landmarks. It stops briefly at the **Bang Sai Handicrafts Centre** created by Queen Sirikit to preserve ancient arts, and **Bang Pa-in**, the former Summer Palace. A sumptuous buffet lunch is served on board. You continue to Ayutthaya for a tour of some of the most important monuments.

Bang Pa-in

The return to Bangkok is via an air-conditioned coach arriving at 6pm. Alternatively, you can take the coach to Ayutthaya and return by boat; a better choice because you then have an evening view of Bangkok from the river. Make your bookings at the Oriental Hotel. Tel: 233-0400 or 236-0420 ext 3133.

A similar hotel transfer, sightseeing and lunch inclusive deal is possible on the slightly more affordable *River Sun* cruiser (Tel: 266-9316). Guests are

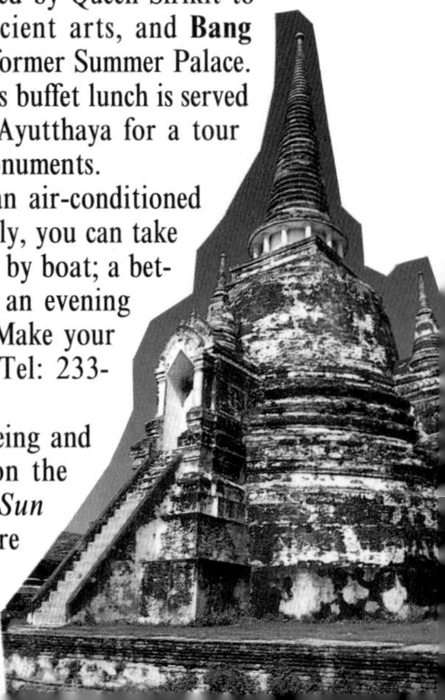

Ancient Ayutthaya

driven by coach to Ayutthaya for sightseeing and sail back, disembarking at the River City Shopping Complex.

The tour serves as a good introduction to the wonders of the city. If you decide to return later for a longer visit, there is a frequent train service from Bangkok's Hualampong Station, and several good hotels on the outskirts of town including the Thong-Inn. Hardy walkers will find Ayutthaya a challenge. Others may prefer to hire a trishaw to visit the key sites. Include the **Chao Sam Phraya Museum** and the new **Ayutthaya Museum** in your itinerary. The latter offers video presentations of the city's history while the former holds some of its art treasures.

Carved stone faces, Ayutthaya

7. River Kwai Bridge

A one-day journey by rail along the Death Railway to the legendary Bridge on the River Kwai.

The tragic story of the Death Railway has been told both in a book and in the memorable David Lean movie *The Bridge on the River Kwai*. Lean filmed in Sri Lanka although after seeing the beautiful scenery of the upper Kwai, one is tempted to ask 'Why?'

'Kwai' or, more properly, 'Khwae' is a designation rather than a name; it means 'branch' of the Mae Klong River. There are two branches, the Khwae Noi (Small Branch) and the Khwae Yai (Large Branch). They are remembered by thousands of Allied soldiers who, as prisoners of war after the fall of Indonesia and Singapore, were forced to build a railway that would link Thailand (which had capitulated to Japanese forces) to Burma so that the Japanese Army could pursue their war against the British forces in India.

The Japanese were brutal taskmasters in a harsh landscape. Beatings, disease, and undernourishment led to the deaths of more than 60,000 Allied soldiers and some 200,000 Asian conscripted labourers. As one author has noted, it amounted to a 'life for every sleeper' (railway tie). If you have the time, it is worthwhile staying for several days, hiking in the bamboo forests, rafting down the river, sleeping in houseboats, or travelling to the **Three Pagoda Pass** on the Burmese border. If planning a journey to the border, do ask about the security situation as there is sporadic fighting between Burmese and Karen soldiers.

The alternative is a one-day trip arranged by the State Railways of Thailand. The train departs Bangkok's Hualampong Station at 6.35am and stops for 40 minutes at **Nakhon Pathom** so you may

The infamous River Kwai Bridge

climb **Phra Pathom Chedi**, the world's tallest Buddhist monument at 127m (417ft). It then continues through the Thai countryside to **Kanchanaburi**, and on to the Bridge just north of town for a walk-across and photos; try to look beyond the commercialization of the area and, instead, visualise the difficult conditions in which the POWs toiled.

The pedestrian walkway over the bridge is not as unsafe as it looks; niches between the spans provide a refuge in case a train happens along. The train then continues up the creaking wooden trestles along the base of a tall limestone cliff, before ending at the terminus at **Nam Tok** for lunch.

You have 2½ hours at Nam Tok to swim in the pond below the waterfall or walk in the jungle. The train returns to Kanchanaburi for a visit to the **Allied Cemetery** holding the POWs who died building the bridge. The train pulls into Hualampong Station at 7.30pm. The ticket includes lunch and refreshments. Book at the Hualampong Station.

8. Petchburi and the Beaches of Hua Hin and Cha-am

A stop at the hilltop Khao Wang palace to break a picturesque train ride and then to two superb beaches.

Trains leave Bangkok's Hualampong Station at 9am for the three-hour journey south to Petchburi and Hua Hin. There are air-conditioned buses which connect Bangkok with the resorts in Hua Hin but the train ride is infinitely more interesting.

The soaring chedi of Khao Wang Palace

Get off at **Petchburi** first, famed for its palace, **Khao Wang**, perched on a hill at the entrance to the city. Built as a retreat by King Mongkut (1851–68), the monarch caricatured in *The King and I*, it has recently been restored.

A cable car ascends the northern flank of the hill, eliminating the arduous climb but you must hire a minibus to get to and from the train station. A steep path lined with fragrant frangipani trees leads past the elephant stables to the main halls, which combine European and Chinese architectural styles. The rooms enjoy a superb view of the surrounding countryside

Room with a view, Khao Wang

and catch the stiff breezes that blow from the sea 16km (10 miles) away. Towering above the other buildings is an observatory where the King indulged in a passion for astronomy.

Catch the train departing Petchburi at 5.36pm, arriving in Hua Hin at 6.38pm. Buses and taxis run between the railway station and beach resorts in Hua Hin and Cha-am.

Limber up and ride at Hua Hin

For half a century, **Hua Hin** has reigned as Thailand's royal playground. King Bhumibol's palace is located on the northern end of the beach. For ordinary mortals, there is a wide beach and a quieter atmosphere than that of Pattaya or Phuket.

The town has some superb beach hotels and fine seafood dining in stilt restaurants along the waterfront. Even if you don't stay at the handsome **Sofitel Railway Hotel** (1 Damnernkasem Road, Tel: 512-021/2), stop for a morning coffee or its excellent buffet breakfast. There is also a beautiful 18-hole golf course near the railway station. On the beach, boys offer for rent catamarans, windsurf boards, parasails, water-skiing equipment, and ponies by the hour.

Cha-am to the north (25km) offers less antiquity but similar accommodations along a beautiful beach.

Chiang Mai

When the Central Plains begin to swelter, many Thais flee to Chiang Mai to enjoy the cooler temperatures and green hills. Chiang Mai is regarded as the cultural centre of Thailand with numerous art studios creating a variety of wood, ceramic, lacquer artifacts and other crafts. Isolated from Bangkok until linked by the railway in the 1920s, Chiang Mai developed its own culture called 'Lanna' which was heavily influenced by Lao art and, in part, by Burmese traditions. The result is a wealth of ornate teak or stucco-covered *wats* quite unlike those found elsewhere in Thailand.

Chiang Mai is for the more adventurous traveller. Visitors normally spend a few days exploring the temples and the markets and then head into the hills to trek to hilltribe villages, ride elephants through the jungles, and float down rivers on bamboo rafts. Chiang Mai also serves as the gateway to ancient kingdoms like Lamphun, Lampang, Chiang Rai, and Chiengsaen, and picturesque towns like Mae Hong Son, Mae Salong, Chom Thong and others. Buses serve these outer areas but those preferring independent travel can opt to rent jeeps or motorcycles for their journeys. There are hotels, guesthouses and restaurants in each of the main towns. In reading the following itineraries, please note that 'H' means 'Highway No.' i.e. 'H108' means 'Highway 108'. Similarly, 'KM' refers to the number painted on the roadside kilometre posts.

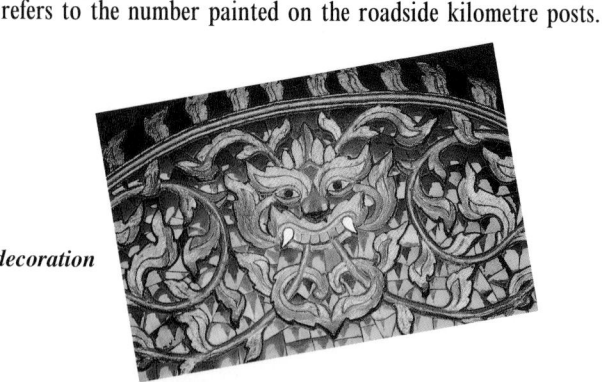

Temple decoration

Monasteries, Hmong village and Doi Suthep temple

Explore four old monasteries by trishaw, ascend a sacred mountain, visit a Hmong village and a royal palace. Then enjoy a riverside dinner and indulge in some nighttime shopping.

An exploration of Chiang Mai begins with a hearty breakfast. Dine at your hotel or ride a trishaw to **Riverview Lodge**, 25 Charoenprathet Road, for breakfast in a riverside garden. Then begin what will be a long but interesting day.

Hardy walkers can cover the 2-km (1-mile) route on foot. Alternatively, flag down a *samlor* (pedal trishaw) or a *tuk-tuk* (motorized trishaw). Tell the driver you want to hire him for three hours to visit the Chedi Luang, Pan Tao, Phra Singh and Chiang Mun *wats*.

The sheer size of **Wat Chedi Luang** makes it one of Chiang Mai's most impressive wats. Step through the entrance gate from Phrapoklao Road, and note the tall gum tree on the left. Legend says that when it falls, so will Chiang Mai. Shaded by its boughs is a city pil-

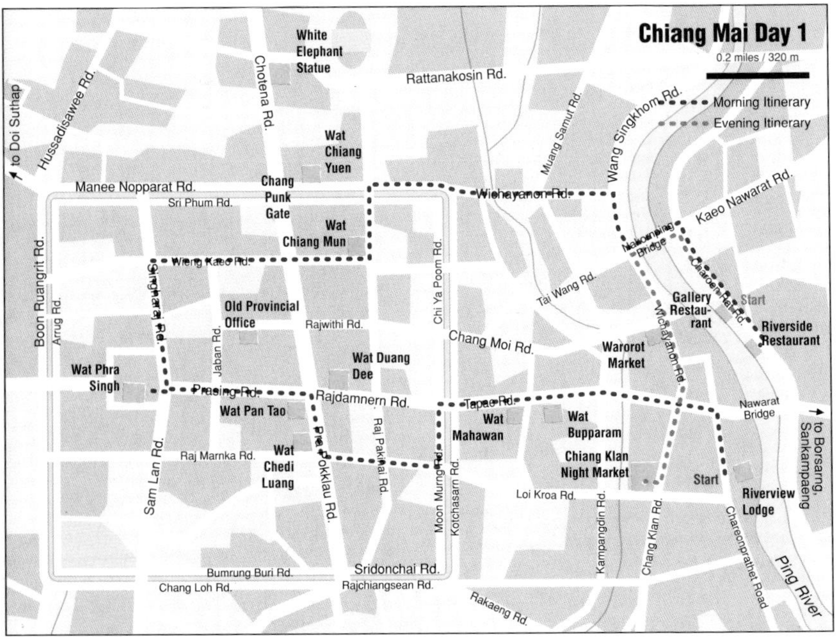

Chiang Mai Day 1

0.2 miles / 320 m

• • • • Morning Itinerary
○ ○ ○ ○ Evening Itinerary

(Map labels:) to Doi Suthep; Hussadisawee Rd.; Chotena Rd.; White Elephant Statue; Rattanakosin Rd.; Muang Samui Rd.; Wang Singkhom Rd.; Kaeo Nawarat Rd.; Manee Nopparat Rd.; Sri Phum Rd.; Wat Chiang Yuen; Chang Punk Gate; Wat Chiang Mun; Wiehayanon Rd.; Nakornping Bridge; Boon Ruangrit Rd.; Arrug Rd.; Wieng Kaeo Rd.; Chi Ya Poom Rd.; Tai Wang Rd.; Gallery Restaurant; Start; Riverside Restaurant; Old Provincial Office; Rajwithi Rd.; Chang Moi Rd.; Warorot Market; Wat Phra Singh; Jaban Rd.; Wat Duang Dee; Prasing Rd.; Rajdamnern Rd.; Tapae Rd.; Wat Mahawan; Wat Bupparam; Nawarat Bridge; Sam Lan Rd.; Wat Pan Tao; Raj Pakhai Rd.; Chiang Klan Night Market; Start; Raj Marnka Rd.; Wat Chedi Luang; Pokklau Rd.; Moon Muang Rd.; Kotchasarn Rd.; Loi Kroa Rd.; Kampangdin Rd.; Chang Klan Rd.; Riverview Lodge; Charoenprathet Road; Ping River; Bumrung Buri Rd.; Sridonchai Rd.; Chang Loh Rd.; Rajchiangsean Rd.; Rakaeng Rd.; to Borsang, Sankampaeng

Anointing the Buddha, Wat Chedi Luang

lar like those that mark the geographic centre of Thai towns; its spirits watch over the city's inhabitants.

The *wat*'s most impressive structure is the huge *chedi* (stupa) at the rear. Built in 1401 by King Saeng Muang Ma, it was raised to 86m (282ft) by King Tilokaraja, builder of Wat Chedi Jet Yod, in 1454. A massive earthquake in 1545 shattered the upper portion, reducing it to 42m (138ft). Recent renovation has robbed it of its atmosphere but it is still impressive. Exit Chedi Luang, walk down the street and enter the first gateway on the left to **Wat Pan Tao**. Its teak *viharn* with its crimson pillars and golden peacock framed by golden serpents is a masterpiece of Lanna art. The interior is less interesting but still worth examining.

Even from a distance, **Wat Phra Singh** is impressive. Situated at the T-junction of Rajdamnern and Singharaj roads, its *viharn* is superbly proportioned. Like many Lanna temples, its balustrade is a *naga* (dragon) with a *makara* emerging from its mouth, a motif found in Cambodian monuments.

Exit the *viharn* and turn left to the beautiful *ho trai* (library for Buddhist scriptures) with its tranquil stucco angels. Running at right angles behind the *viharn* is a beautiful wooden *bot* with a superb stucco and gold entrance. Behind it is an elephant-supported *chedi* built by King Pha Yu in 1345 to hold the ashes of his father, King Kam Fu.

The most beautiful of Phra Singh's building is the famous **Phra Viharn Laikram** to the left of the *chedi*. As with all *bots*, its sacred boundary is defined by six stone *bai sema*, or boundary stones. Although built in 1811, it embodies the finest Lanna architectural traditions. Intricately-carved stucco door frames compete in beauty with the doors themselves. In-

Door mural, Wat Chiang Mun

side, water-damaged 19th-century murals on the right wall tell the story of Saengthong, a mythical Thai hero. The left wall is devoted to Suphannahong, a mythical swan seen frequently in northern art and architecture.

Go down Singaharaj Road, turn right into Wieng Kaeo Road and cross Phra Pokhlao Road. At the next corner on the left is the *wat* you're looking for. **Wat Chiang Mun** on Rajaphinkai Road is the oldest monastery within the city walls. Completed when the city was consecrated in 1296, its name translates as 'power of the city'. Tradition says that King Mengrai lived in its courtyard while he was building his new capital.

Its central building, a 19th-century Lanna-style *viharn* is decorated with the three-headed elephant god, Erawan. Look for the superbly carved teak gable panels. Inside are several handsome bronze Buddha images from the Lanna and U-thong (15th century) periods. Ask a monk to unlock the doors. The murals of the right-hand *viharn* chronicle Buddha's life with the *chadoks* (previous incarnations of the Buddha) appearing in the lower panels. The altar holds Chiang Mai's two most sacred Buddha images: the small crystal **Phra Setang Khamani** on the left, dating back to 1281, brings rain and protects the city from fire; the finely-carved **Phra Sila** on the right was reputedly brought from India around AD1000.

Walk to the rear of the compound. Reflecting Sri Lankan influences, the 15th-century *chedi* appears to be supported by 15 brick and stucco elephants, an architectural device found in several Sukhothai and Kampaengphet *chedis*.

Left of the *chedi* is the *ho trai*, a masterpiece of Thai wood carving and lacquer decoration. In its small museum are lacquer manuscript cabinets, Buddha images, pipes, and old Thai money.

In the far left-hand corner of the courtyard, the plain wooden doors of the *bot* open onto some superb Lanna and U-thong period bronze Buddha images.

Your last trishaw stop is the **Riverside Restaurant** on Charoenrat Road to enjoy a Thai or European lunch while taking in views of the city from the left bank of the Ping River.

Chiang Mai Day 1 Afternoon
2.5 miles / 4 km

The afternoon takes you up **Doi Suthep**, the city's most sacred mountain. Minibuses (one leaves from Tapae Road in front of the Bangkok Bank every 10 minutes for Doi Suthep, Phuping and Doi Pui) climb the long and winding road from the western end of Huay Kaew Road just past the zoo, but it is better to use your own car or motorcycle. Drive 12km (7½ miles) to the parking lot of Wat Doi Suthep, but instead of stopping, continue up the road on the left through pine forests to Phuping Palace, 4km (2½ miles) farther on.

Phuping, the royal family's Chiang Mai residence, serves as a command post for development projects in northern Thai and hill-tribe villages. When the royal family is not in residence, the beau-

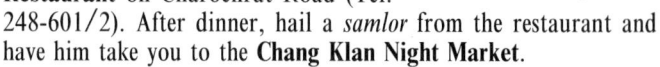

tiful flower gardens are opened to the public, Friday through Sunday from 8.30am to 4.30pm.

Continue 3km (1¾ miles) to the Hmong village of **Doi Pui**. The village lives on tourism and seems to be little more than a hilltribe theme park. It does, however, provide a glimpse of hill village life; in the winter, the hollyhock gardens are beautiful. There is a small museum holding household implements. Note: if you take a photograph of a Hmong, you will very likely be asked for money.

About 4pm, backtrack to **Wat Phra That Doi Suthep**, Chiang Mai's most famous temple. A funicular railway carries you to the summit but resist the temptation to ride it. You accumulate more merit (and a healthy workout) by climbing the 210 steps (304 if you count from the parking lot).

Legend says that a monk named Sumana placed half of a Buddha relic on an elephant's back and set it loose; wherever the elephant stopped, a temple would be built to house the gem.

Well, the elephant must have had a perverse streak, because instead of stopping at an easy site, it began climbing a hill and all the way up to the 1,073m (3,521ft) level. There, the Wat Phra That Doi Suthep was built.

Remove your shoes and climb to the inner sanctuary. Shorts are taboo but vendors near the entrance rent sarongs for 10 baht. The upper courtyard is dominated by a dazzling gilded brass *chedi* which gleams in the afternoon sun. Small gilded Buddha images cap the spiked fence pickets and peer from odd corners. Framed photographs honour a long-deceased rooster that pecked at the feet of ignorant tourists who entered the courtyard wearing shoes.

At 5pm, monks gather in the western *viharn* to chant their prayers. After listening to the ethereal murmurings, exit the courtyard and turn left. Strike the big bronze bells for good luck and walk to the balustrade to watch dusk descend on Chiang Mai far below.

Return to your hotel and after freshening up, dine amidst tall trees overlooking the Ping River at **The Gallery Restaurant** on Charoenrat Road (Tel:

Guardian of Doi Suthep

248-601/2). After dinner, hail a *samlor* from the restaurant and have him take you to the **Chang Klan Night Market**.

The market has evolved from a cluster of handicraft stalls to a shopping mall that threatens to take over the city centre. Browse among the stalls for a bit of haggling and shopping, and look out for artists who for a small fee will paint flowers and your name on your camera or cigarette lighter.

9. Borsang Handicraft Tour

Spend a morning observing how Thai artisans create some of Chiang Mai's exquisite handicrafts.

After breakfast, catch red and white Bus No. 2259 that travels east on Charoenmuang Road to **Borsang**. Or better still, hire a *tuk-tuk* for the entire morning. You will be visiting a variety of shops which will welcome you to watch as young craftsmen create the art objects for which the city is famed. As you will quickly discover, the range of items is quite broad although the quality varies according to the individual craftsman. There is no guided tour; you simply wander at will. Each shop has a showroom but you are under no obligation to buy. If you do buy, the shops can arrange air or sea shipping at reasonable rates.

The following shops lie along the 9-km (5½-mile) road to Borsang beginning at the Superhighway intersection.

Napa Lacquerware at 8/2 Sankampaeng Road (KM3.2), Tel: 243-039, specialises in lacquerware. Northern lacquerware involves gold leaf designs on glossy black, or green and black designs on a dark red base. Betel boxes, serving trays, and jewellery boxes are created from bamboo and overlaid with lacquer. Napa also covers its containers in crushed, dyed eggshell mosaics. Among the most popular items are the gold and black lacquer boxes but check carefully to ensure that the design is cleanly rendered.

The **Pon Art Gallery** at 35/3 Moo 3 (KM5.8), Tel: 338-361, comprises a number of Thai-style houses crammed with an astounding variety of Thai and Burmese wooden gods and whimsical beasts which are ideal as decorative items. The neo-antiques are produced at Baan Tawai, south of Chiang Mai at Hang Dong (worth a side trip if you

The final touches to a lacquerware vase

Tools of the woodcarving trade

have time), and sold here. Even if you have no desire to own a mirror-mosaic dragon or a red Ganesh elephant god, it is fun to browse for an hour or two.

Lanna Thai, No. 79 Sankampaeng Road (KM6.1), Tel: 338-015/7, produces both antique and modern silverware and hilltribe jewellery. The silver content is low but the workmanship is good and the variety of items and prices ensure you will find a small gift to your liking.

At **Shinawatra**, 145/1–2 Sankampaeng Road (KM7.1), Tel: 338-053/8, observe how silkworms fed on mulberry leaves produce filaments that are woven into Thai silk and cut into garments. The air-conditioned showroom carries printed silk items like scarfs and pillowcases. It also sells Thai silk in lengths to be cut into suits and gowns by tailors in Chiang Mai and Bangkok.

Chamchuree Lapidary, 166/1 Sankampaeng Road (KM7.5), Tel: 338-631, carves Burmese jade into pendants and jewellery. The nephrite and jadeite comes from across the border in Burma; you save money by being so near to the source.

Arts & Crafts Chiang Mai, 172 Sankampaeng Road (KM7.8), Tel: 331-977, casts bronze deities and animals which can be used indoors and outdoors. The items are normally clad in brass skins to make them gleam.

Chiang Mai Sudalak, 99/9 Sankampaeng Road (KM8.2), Tel: 338-006, carves northern timber into furniture and home decor items. Items range from beds and writing desks to chopping boards and trivets. A number of natural and glossy finishes are offered, the most popular being a lightly-brushed paint which gives a piece an antique look.

The **Umbrella Making Centre**, 111/2 Sankampaeng Road (KM9), Tel: 338-324, combines bamboo, string and *sah* paper (made from the bark of the paper mulberry tree) into umbrellas that are a marvel of engineering. This is Chiang Mai's most famous product and ranges in size from parasols to huge patio umbrellas, and in decoration from plain to outrageously ornate.

Prem Pracha, on Sankampaeng Road at the Borsang intersection (KM9), Tel: 338-540, skilfully moulds celadon, ceramic, blue and

Ceramics painting at Prem Pracha

white porcelain, earthenware and *bencharong* (five-colour porcelain) into pots, lamp stands, and bowls. If you are looking for attractive and inexpensive gifts, this is the place to shop.

For lunch, return to the KM4 post, turn left and drive about 200m (656ft) to **Baan Suan** which serves authentic Thai food in a lovely, cool garden.

10. Elephant Camp and Chiang Dao Caves

Get off to an early start and watch elephants work and then raft down the Ping River. Continue to the Chiang Dao Caves and if you're feeling fit enough, make the steep climb into the caves.

A bus leaves Chang Puak Gate Bus Station at 7am for Chiang Dao. Get off at KM56 at the **Chiang Dao Elephant Camp**. Shows start at 9 and 10am.

Elephants bathe in the Ping River and then move huge teak logs as if they were toothpicks, just like they have for centuries in the northern forests. Take a short elephant ride around the grounds for a unique vantage view of the scenery.

Enjoy a snack or soft drink at the open air restaurants perched over the Ping River before negotiating with a boatmen for a 4½-kilometre (3-mile) ride on a bamboo raft down the **Ping** to **Tha Rua**. There, walk to the Chiang Mai-Fang Highway and take the same bus that brought you to the Elephant Camp to the **Chiang Dao Caves**. If you have parked a car or motorcycle at the Elephant Camp, catch a bahtbus to retrieve it and then head up the highway to Chiang Dao. About 500m (1,641ft) beyond the town, turn left and drive for 5km (3 miles) through villages and tobacco fields to the caves.

Running 1,470m (4,823ft) into the mountain, the caves comprise a series of rooms reached by climbing stairs and a ladder. A guide with a lantern will accompany you for 20 baht to view Buddha statues. The trip is somewhat strenuous, so attempt it only if you have sufficient energy.

Return to your vehicle, stop for a welcome drink under the tamarind trees and then drive to Chiang Mai. Several shops along the road sell farm implements, fishing baskets, and village utensils that make unusual, lightweight gifts.

Taking an elephant for a ride

11. Old Homes and Museums

A visit to two old-style Thai houses and lunch in a third.

Chiang Mai is filled with beautiful old teak homes. Several of these unique houses with their wealth of artifacts offer glimpses of life as it was lived when the world moved at a slower pace. The **Lanna Folk Museum** is one which can be easily reached by bicycle or *samlor*. Leave the Sridonchai Road, turning onto Wua Lai Road. The museum sits 1km (½ mile) down on the left, about 500m (1,641ft) before Wua Lai's intersection with the Superhighway.

The 130-year-old Lanna-style **Galae House** in the gardens occupied a site on the banks of the Ping River before it was moved to its present site several years ago. With its collection of antique household utensils and farm equipment, it serves as an ethnological museum. Open 10am to 4pm daily (closed Thursday).

The proud owner of Banyen Museum

Continue south on Wua Lai, and cross the Superhighway intersection. The **Banyen Museum** sits on the far left-hand corner. The museum is a sprawling complex created by one of Chiang Mai's pioneer antique dealers, Mrs Banyen. Housed in the central building on stilts, the museum holds superbly carved wooden gables and other objects from northern *wats*. More fun for the visitor is a stroll through the gardens to see newer wood carvings which are for sale. Their appeal lies in the setting as much as their artistry. Open 8am to 4.30pm (closed Sundays).

For lunch, take a *samlor* or cycle east (towards the river) on the Superhighway for one kilometre. A few metres before reaching the bridge over the Ping River, turn left. The road winds for about 500m (1641ft) before straightening out to head for **Chan Klang Road**. At that point, look for a red postal box on the right; many cars will be turning here as well. Follow them past the turning across the Mengrai Bridge. Whimsically called **Once Upon a Time**, the restaurant is located on the right about 500m (1641ft) north of the Mengrai Bridge intersection, at 38/2 Charoenprathet Road (Tel: 274-932). Enjoy European and Thai lunch on the balcony of an old wooden house decorated with Lanna art.

EXCURSIONS

12. Mae Sa Valley

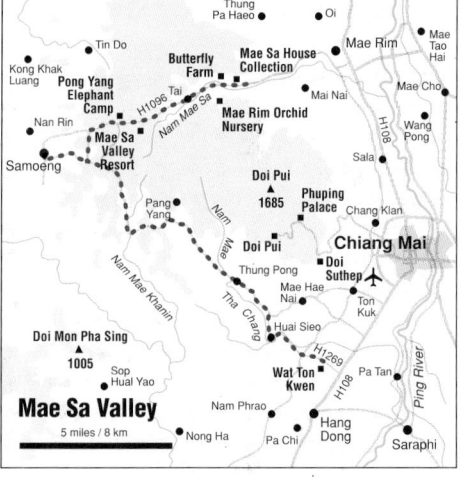

Mae Sa Valley

5 miles / 8 km

Travel on winding roads through beautiful valleys, stopping at an elephant camp, an orchid nursery, a butterfly farm, and an old museum along the way. You need a car or motorcycle for this full day excursion.

Drive south on H108, 6½km (4 miles) to KM10, and turn right onto H1269. At KM2.1, turn left down a narrow road to **Wat Ton Kwen**. This peaceful little temple amid date palm trees is a lovely example of Lanna architecture. Its wooden *bot*, guarded by a pair of handsome stucco *nagas* (dragons), is surrounded on three sides by an open cloister whose tiled roof holds some interesting mythical animals.

Return to H1269 and turn left. The highway runs through green valleys and passes behind Doi Suthep. At KM38 (there is a police booth on the left) drop down the hill into **Samoeng**, a pretty valley town with some lovely, tree-shaded streets. Stop at an open-air restaurant for an iced coffee and then return to KM38, turning left onto H1096. It is 31½km (20 miles) to the Chiang Mai-Fang highway but many treats lie along the way.

On the left, several kilometres beyond the intersection, is the **Pong Yang Elephant Camp**. Its elephant shows at 8am and 9.40am are inferior to that at Chiang Dao but they offer a good half-hour elephant ride into the hills. If you have time, take the two-hour ride up the valley.

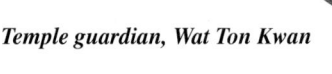

Temple guardian, Wat Ton Kwan

Orchids at Mae Rim

On the right, 1km (½ mile) down H1096, is the **Mae Sa Valley Resort** whose manicured gardens sit in sharp contrast to the wild beauty of the surrounding jungle. In the winter, the flowers in full bloom are a pretty sight.

Of more interest to flower lovers is the **Mae Rim Orchid Nursery** farther down the valley. The shop sells orchid seedlings with instructions for their care; be sure that your country allows them past customs. Wander in clouds of butterflies at the spacious, net-covered garden of the **Butterfly Farm** further down on the left. The **Mae Sa Collection House** farther on holds family heirlooms, including a clock that runs backwards and an early motorcycle. To return, drive on H1096 another 4½km (3 miles) to H108, and turn right; it is 16km (10 miles) to Chiang Mai via the Chang Puak Gate.

13. Mae Hong Son

You need two days for this trip, staying overnight in a picturesque town on the Burmese border.

Its Burmese-style temples and valley setting make **Mae Hong Son**, west of Chiang Mai, one of the North's most beautiful towns. An inexpensive round-trip THAI ticket from Chiang Mai makes even a short trip worthwhile.

On arrival and check in at your hotel, spend time absorbing the atmosphere at **Jong Kum Lake** and its two wats: **Wat Jong Klang** and **Wat Jong Kum**. Both are fine examples of Burmese architecture with their tiny roofs stacked one atop the other and the filigree fretwork along their eaves. The gilded *chedi* is a prime example of Burmese design with its terraced base, squat body, and spire of discs rising to a delicate crown.

Wat Jong Klang holds a famous collection of statues depicting scenes from the Vessantara Chadok, Buddha's last incarnation before he reached enlightenment. His life is also depicted in glass paintings. In them, a selfless monarch is exiled from his kingdom for giving a sacred elephant to an enemy king. In the afternoon, walk to **Wat Phra Non** and its 12-metre (39-ft) long **Reclining Buddha** statue, depicting him

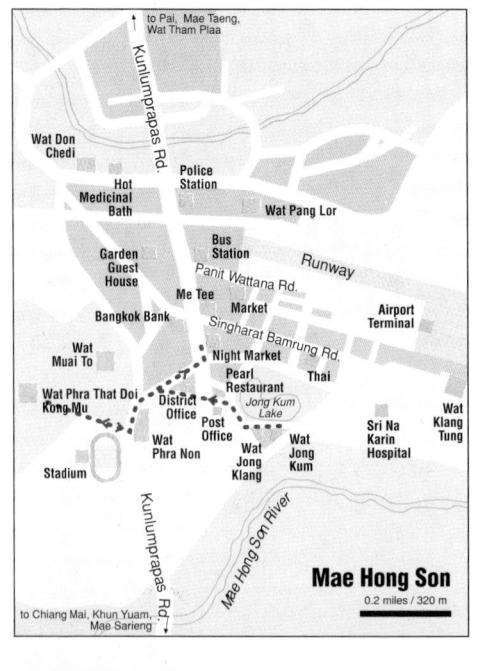

Mae Hong Son

0.2 miles / 320 m

to Pai, Mae Taeng, Wat Tham Plaa

Kunlumprapas Rd.

Wat Don Chedi

Hot Medicinal Bath

Police Station

Wat Pang Lor

Garden Guest House

Bus Station

Panit Wattana Rd.

Runway

Me Tee

Bangkok Bank

Market

Singharat Bamrung Rd.

Airport Terminal

Wat Muai To

Night Market

Pearl Restaurant

Thai

Wat Phra That Doi Kong Mu

District Office

Jong Kum Lake

Post Office

Wat Jong Klang

Wat Jong Kum

Sri Na Karin Hospital

Wat Klang Tung

Wat Phra Non

Stadium

Kunlumprapas Rd.

Mae Hong Son River

to Chiang Mai, Khun Yuam, Mae Sarieng

at death. Cross the road and ascend a steep stairway to **Wat Phra That Doi Kong Mu**. It can also be reached by road. The *wat* comprises of two beautiful *chedis* and a superb view of the valley. From the parapet, watch the sun set over the town.

If you spend the night, walk to the **night market** on Kunlumprapas Road for a dinner of Thai vendor food, or dine at the **Pearl Restaurant** on Chamnan Sathit Road near the lake. Shop for crafts at **Singharat Bamrung Road**; the **La-or Shop** has a wide selection. Before retiring, stroll to the lake to enjoy Wat Jong Klang chedi's lights winking on the lake surface.

14. Hilltribe Treks

Trek into the hills and stay in a hilltribe village.

A highlight of a visit to Chiang Mai can be a stay of between two and five days in a hilltribe village. These are not primitive headhunters of Borneo but a rather civilized people living in somewhat primitive conditions. Many of the hilltribes have only recently been weaned away from growing opium, and now cultivate a wide variety of garden crops. Village accommodation will be spartan; at times with only sleeping bags on woven bamboo floors for beds. Meals are basic – rice with meat and vegetables – but are tasty.

In recent years, trekking has become so popular that tourists are having a deleterious effect on the environment and on hilltribe values. If you want to keep your impact to a minimum, travel with a reputable trekking agency. It is difficult to recommend one over another as the quality of the trek depends on the guide, and guides frequently change companies. Shop around and ask questions about the proprietors' sensitivity to tribal customs, and the size of your trekking group; more than six persons is too large. Look for a trek that visits one or two tribal groups, not one which skips through several villages in rapid succession. Seek an agency that employs tribesmen as guides. Trekking companies line **Tapae** and **Chaiyaphum** roads.

Hmong hilltribe women

Popular trekking routes lie north of Chiang Mai and in the hills around Chiang Rai. Some treks combine village stays with elephant rides and raft rides. Dress casually but cover your skin from the sun. If agencies don't provide sleeping bags and mosquito nets, buy them in shops along **Manee Noparat Road**. Carry a daypack with a change of clothes and toilet paper wrapped in plastic bags, and a canteen rather than disposable plastic water bottles. The North is surprisingly dry during the winter so carry chapstick and moisturiser. Note: Western women often ride rafts topless. Not only is this culturally insensitive, it is asking for trouble.

NORTHEAST

The Northeast is generally ignored by tourists, and without justification. Its culture is akin to that of Laos and is less formal (and, some say, more fun) than that of other regions of Thailand. It also holds a wealth of superb architecture dating from the 11th and 12th centuries, testimony to the westward expansion of the empire of the great rulers of Angkor Wat. Because it is relatively untouched by tourists, the Northeast has a freshness, and its people an openness not found in other areas of Thailand. Once they have discovered it, many visitors prefer the Northeast and its relaxed lifestyle to other sections of Thailand. Near Korat (Nakhon Ratchasima) are several Khmer temples which rival those of Ayutthaya or Angkor Wat. Further east is the Khmer temple of Khao Phra Viharn, which officially belongs to Cambodia.

EXCURSIONS

15. Exploring the Northeast

Take a one or two-day trip to Korat to visit the sanctuary Prasat Phanom Wan, the ruins of Phimai, and a Khmer hilltop temple.

On Monday and Saturday, you can make a one-day trip to Korat from Bangkok, flying THAI at 7 or 7.15am and returning on the 8.10pm flight. Alternatively, the express sleeper train leaves at 12.15am, arriving in Bangkok at 5.20am. If you

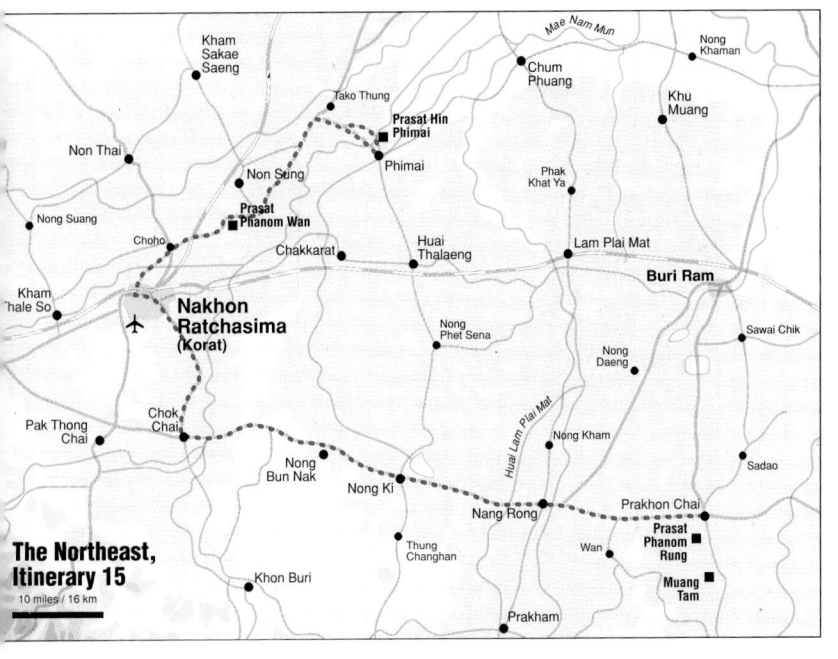

The Northeast,
Itinerary 15

10 miles / 16 km

plan to stay overnight, THAI has a flight that departs at 6.30pm while airconditioned trains depart Bangkok at 10.15am arriving at 2.20pm at Korat. Hire a hotel taxi for the day. Two of the sites, Prasat Phanom Wan and Phimai, lie within close reach of Korat. Drive 14km (9 miles) north on H2. Turn right onto a dirt road that, 4km (2½ miles) later, reaches the remote sanctuary of **Prasat Phanom Wan**.

In this 11th-century sandstone ruins are found the corbelled roofs, delicately carved lintels, *prangs* (spires) and false windows with stone mullions that echo the grandeur of Angkor Wat. Unlike most Khmer ruins in the Northeast, the central sanctuary is still used for worship. Behind its vaulted entrance, the original sanctuary is filled with recent Buddha images of different styles, most of them covered with gold leaf. Make a small cash donation to support the upkeep of the site.

Khmer ruins, Phimai

To reach Phimai, continue north on H2 for another 20km (12½ miles), turning right for 10km (6 miles) to the ruins of **Phimai**, Thailand's best-preserved Khmer ruin. Built by the last of the great Angkorian monarchs, King Jayavarman VII

An elaborately carved lintel at Prasat Phanom Rung

(1181–1201), its original entrance gate still stands at the end of Phimai's present main street. Wander through its sanctuaries, pausing to inspect lintels, and the marvellous sense of perspective the architects achieved. Near Moun River Bridge is an open-air museum displaying some of Phimai's superbly-carved lintels and statues.

Before leaving Phimai, stop at **Sai Ngam**, 1km (½ mile) east of the temple. Its enormous dense canopy shelters several shrines dedicated to spirits. Return to Korat for lunch and then drive south on H24 to Chok Chai and then east on H218. After 80km (50 miles) the road forks; take the right fork and proceed another 18km (11 miles) to Ban Ta Ko. Turn right at the sign for **Prasat Phanom Rung**. Follow the road to Ban Wan and bear left to reach the Khmer hilltop temple that historians believe was an important outpost between Angkor and Phimai during the 11th and 12th century.

The Khmers were masters in marrying site to architecture, and few complexes can match Prasat Phanom Rung's beauty. They liked long, sweeping staircases and esplanades to convey grandeur. Running along the spine of the hill and interrupted by landings, the monumental stairway exudes the mass and power typical of Khmer design. At the summit is the recently restored sanctuary whose main *prang*, galleries and chapels reflect the geometric precision of Angkorian architecture with symmetrical doors and windows, and antechapels facing the four cardinal points. Enjoy the view.

16. A Peek into Cambodia: Khao Phra Viharn

A climb up the magnificent cliffside Khmer temple complex of Khao Phra Viharn. Weekends only.

Khmer architects were masters of hillside settings and this is one of their masterpieces. Long stairways ascend a ridge from shrine to shrine. At the summit is a stupendous view of the Cambodian plain, 500m (1,641ft) below you.

By an anomaly of history, **Khao Phra Viharn** officially belongs to Cambodia but can only be reached from Thailand. The complex comprises a series of stairways and landings with the shells of Hindu temples later used by Buddhists after Khmer monarchs of the 12th century converted to the new religion. Halfway up are ceremonial ponds which also served as sources of water, an important feature of Khmer architecture. Further up are beautiful stone buildings with intricately-carved stone window mullions and panels. Long, covered cloisters convey much of the atmosphere of former days. At the summit, look for the bunker dug by Khmer soldiers who used the complex as a watchtower during the incessant war of the past two decades.

State Railways of Thailand (SRT) offers a weekend trip, but be warned: it is gruelling, involving a climb in the hot sun up the long slope and an overnight bus ride.

A special train leaves Bangkok at 9.25am on Saturday and arrives in Ubon at 5.50pm. After an overnight hotel stay, ride an air-conditioned bus to the temple for the climb to the top. After visiting neighbouring sites, you return to Ubon and at 8.20pm, board an air-conditioned bus

The imposing Khao Phra Viharn

for Bangkok, arriving in at 5.35am on Monday. Book at Bangkok's Hualampong Train Station. Remember to take along your passport. Check with the SRT first as security problems along the Cambodian border means that Khao Phra Viharn is sometimes off limits to tourists. Tel: 223-0341/8, 223-7010.

Stairway to the temple

Phuket

From a small island known only to tin miners, rubber planters, and fishermen two decades ago, Phuket has blossomed into Asia's premier beach resort, by far outstripping its cousin, Pattaya, on the eastern shore of the Gulf of Thailand. Its appeal lies in its stunning beaches, balmy weather, clear blue waters, and its wealth of activities. Lesser known but equally attractive are its lush green forests, and its multitude of nearby islands which offer spectacular scenery and some of the best reef diving in the world.

Phuket town is essentially a nondescript provisioning centre for the rest of the island but it also holds a wealth of old buildings in several styles, all of which invite exploration. Although most visitors prefer to stay at beach resorts, Phuket town serves as the hub from which to travel to see the other islands. The size of Singapore, Phuket is best explored by rented jeep or motorcycle.

Those in less of a hurry may choose to ride a system of rickety but picturesque buses that ply regular routes to most beaches and to some inland towns. Note: Some of Phuket's beaches have a nasty undertow, especially during the monsoon season. Ask first if you're unsure. If you do get caught in an undertow, lie flat in the water; the waves will eventually carry you to a shallow point where you can regain your footing.

The Phuket coastal beach strip

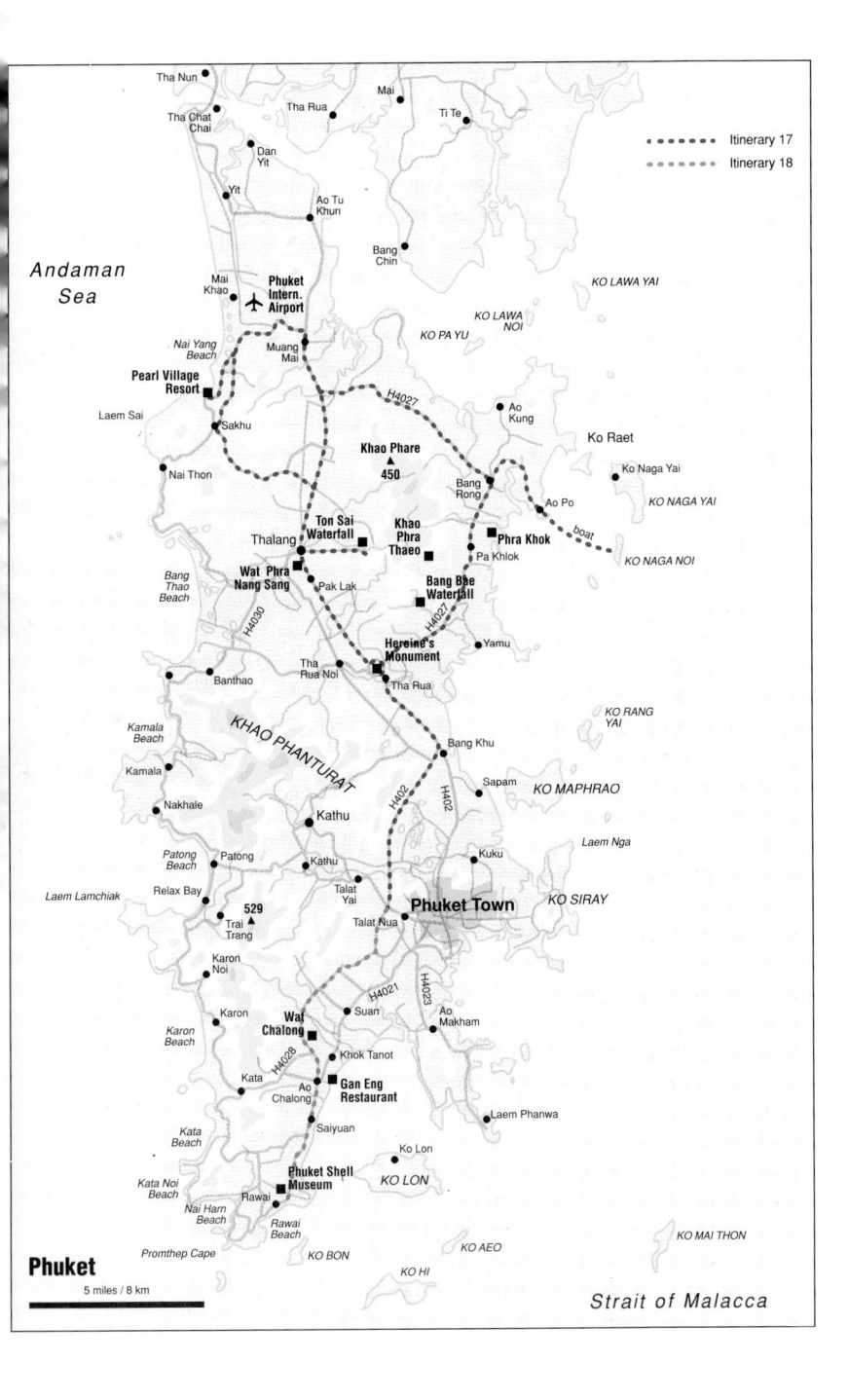

Itinerary 17
Itinerary 18

*Andaman
Sea*

Tha Nun
Tha Chat
Chai
Mai
Tha Rua
Ti Te
Dan
Yit
Ao Tu
Khun
Yit
Bang
Chin
KO LAWA YAI
Mai
Khao
**Phuket
Intern.
Airport**
*Nai Yang
Beach*
Muang
Mai
KO PA YU
*KO LAWA
NOI*
**Pearl Village
Resort**
Laem Sai
Sakhu
H4027
Ao
Kung
Ko Raet
Nai Thon
Khao Phare
▲
450
Bang
Rong
Ko Naga Yai
Ao Po
KO NAGA YAI
**Ton Sai
Waterfall**
**Khao
Phra
Thaeo**
■ **Phra Khok**
*Bang
Thao
Beach*
Thalang
Pa Khlok
boat
KO NAGA NOI
**Wat Phra
Nang Sang**
Pak Lak
**Bang Bae
Waterfall**
H4030
H4027
**Heroine's
Monument**
Yamu
Banthao
Tha
Rua Noi
Tha Rua
*Kamala
Beach*
KHAO PHANTURAT
Bang Khu
*KO RANG
YAI*
Kamala
Sapam
KO MAPHRAO
Nakhale
H402
H402
Kuku
Laem Nga
*Patong
Beach*
Patong
Kathu
Kathu
Laem Lamchiak
Relax Bay
Talat
Yai
Phuket Town
KO SIRAY
529
▲
Trai
Trang
Talat Nua
Karon
Noi
Karon
*Karon
Beach*
**Wat
Chalong**
Suan
H4021
H4023
Ao
Makham
Kata
Khok Tanot
**Gan Eng
Restaurant**
Ao
Chalong
H4028
*Kata
Beach*
Saiyuan
Laem Phanwa
*Kata Noi
Beach*
Rawai
**Phuket Shell
Museum**
Ko Lon
KO LON
*Nai Harn
Beach*
*Rawai
Beach*
Promthep Cape
KO BON
KO AEO
KO HI
KO MAI THON

Phuket

5 miles / 8 km

Strait of Malacca

Beach Safari

Phuket has a multitude of white sandy beaches to satisfy even the most finicky of aficionados. If the beach fronting your resort doesn't meet your expectations (an unlikely event), get a jeep and drive around till you find one

Most visitors prefer to spend their first day or so sunning on the sand, taking occasional dips in the ocean, and discovering the delicious seafood the restaurants offer. More restless travellers may want to set off in search of the perfect beach, of which there are several. At some time during their stay, you should explore all the varied beaches that Phuket offers.

Phuket beaches come in a range of types. Secluded coves and broad strands, deserted or crowded, they share the same powdery sand, warm aquamarine water and palm trees. To discover which one suits you best, rent a jeep or motorcycle and spend a

Rent-an-elephant, Nai Yang beac

day or two as a beach gypsy, exploring Phuket's aquatic offerings. Take along a swimsuit and a towel; you will find restaurants and drinks on each beach. The following are the key beaches and their personalities, running from north to south of the western shore.

With 9km (5½ miles) of snowy white sand, **Mai Khao** (White Wood), north of the airport, is Phuket's longest beach. Construction has been banned here so there are no accommodations, only a few small thatched restaurants.

Shaded by tall pine-like casuarina trees, **Nai Yang** is part of a National Park. There are changing rooms and rustic bungalows for rent. Between November and February, Ridley Sea Turtles crawl ashore at night to lay their eggs The Pearl Village Resort anchors the southern end of this stunning beach.

Bang Thao is occupied by several large hotels but outsiders can find quiet corners of the lagoon in which to relax and swim. **Surin Beach** is undeveloped because it has

อ.กะทู้ 2
KATHU

หาดป่าตอง 6
PA TONG BEACH

60

Karon Beach sunset: leave only footprints behind.

dangerous undertow as does beautiful **Kamala beach**, a fishing village. The northern end of Kamala has some low-cost bungalows.

Patong (Banana Plantation), 15km (9 miles) west of Phuket town, is Phuket's most developed (some would say, overdeveloped) beach with the island's largest concentration of hotels and the widest array of sports facilities, nightlife, shops, and restaurants. If you prefer a busy resort to a quiet hidden beach, this is it.

Just south, **Relax Bay** holds a single hotel, Le Meridien Phuket on a private beach. One of Phuket's loveliest beaches, **Karon** has a treacherous undertow during the monsoon season. Walk its sands and hear them squeak.

Club Med chose **Kata** beach for its second resort in Asia and for good reason. A tall hill separates Kata from **Kata Noi** nestled in a scenic bay whose southern shore offers fine snorkelling.

One of Phuket's loveliest beaches, **Nai Harn** (Lagoon) lies between two banana-treed ridges and faces the setting sun. It is one of the least-developed of the beaches but therein lies its charm.

Sea sports and ... serenity

The foreshore of **Rawai** beach, on Phuket's southernmost tip, is too rocky for swimmers, but at low tide it offers good hunting grounds for shell collectors.

Nai Harn beach jog

PICK & MIX

17. Nature Trail

Explore Phuket's national parks. Take along a towel and swim suit and rent a motorcycle or jeep for this tour.

Although Phuket is known for its beaches, it offers several green pockets of superb beauty. Thus, when you tire of sand and sea, there is a welcome change awaiting you.

Drive on H402 (the airport road) 18½km (11½ miles) north to the old capital city of Thalang. At the traffic lights, turn right and drive down a beautiful 4-km (2½-mile) corridor of rubber trees to

The scenic road to Nai Yang

the Forestry Department checkpost. The fork on the left takes you into **Khao Phra Thaeo National Park** (6am–6pm).

Park and walk the 250-metre (820-ft) trail to **Ton Sai Waterfall**, taking the middle path. In the dry season, the waterfall is barely a trickle but in the monsoon it becomes a torrent. A small restaurant nearby sells soft drinks and snacks.

Refreshed by the icy-cold waters of the waterfall, exit the Park, drive back to Talang and turn right. Head north on Thepkasatri Road (H402) to KM21.4. Turn left onto H4031 and enter a beautiful 1-km (½-mile) stretch of rubber trees that arch over the narrow road. Beyond it are rice paddies filled with lolling water buffaloes.

At KM7, a sign on the left marks the entrance to the **Pearl Village** resort. At the resort entrance, motorcyclists should take the narrow dirt path to the right that bypasses the hotel and exits at **Nai Yang National Park**. If you are driving a car, however, carry on up H4031 for another kilometre, turning left at a blue sign onto a dirt road leading into the park.

Nai Yang sits amidst tall, wispy casuarina trees that fringe a beautiful beach with great swimming; a changing room with showers charges a small fee. Near the northern end is a **Park Visitor Centre** with displays of coral, shells, butterflies, turtles, and other fauna found on Phuket. For overnight stays, the park rents inexpensive bungalows with fans and electricity. Apply at the head-quarters in the middle of the park. Alternatively, stay at the up-market **Pearl Village Resort**.

Giant Ridley Sea Turtles weighing up to 850kg (1,874lb) clamber onto the **Nai Yang beach** each night between November and February. Digging deep holes with their flippers, they lay up to 200 leathery-shelled eggs, instinctual behaviour said to be 90 million years old. Take a flashlight and try not to disturb the turtles labouring at their task.

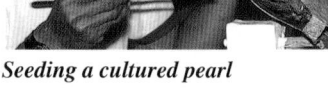

Seeding a cultured pearl

From the park, take the north exit and continue left on H4031 past the airport, rejoining H402 4km (2½ miles) later. Turn left and follow the signs to the 'National Park', beside isolated **Mai Khao** beach. Alternatively, turn right (south) on the H402 and at KM25.5 turn left onto the H4027 to Pa Klok. At KM10.2 on H4027, turn left to **Ao Po** a coastal town a short drive away. Have a soft drink at the seaside coffeeshop. Ao Po tour companies can arrange a boat ride to the **Pearl Farm** on **Naga Noi island** where experts demonstrate how oysters are seeded to produce cultured pearls. The world's largest pearl was cultured here.

From Ao Po, return to H4027 and turn left. At KM8.4, turn right to **Bang Bae Waterfall**. About 1.2km (0.7 miles) down a dirt road is the parking lot. Climb 300m (984ft) to the falls with its series of pools. Beside the parking lot is the intriguing **Gibbon Rehabilitation Project**. Return to H4027. Turn right to the Heroine's Monument. On Fridays, there is a market worth looking at. Turn left and return to Phuket town on H402.

18. Rawai Shell Hunt

Hunt for shells at Rawai and then see them in all their splendour. Morning or afternoon tour, depending on tides.

Drive south on the H4201 to the Chalong junction, passing it and heading 4km (2½ miles) down the H4024 to **Rawai beach**. If the tide is out, venture onto the rocky shoals, listening to the drying stones crackle and pop in the sun. If you are lucky, sea gypsy crab catchers and shell pickers will be prowling on the rocks and you can watch them work.

Turn over a few rocks and look for shells clinging to their undersides. The shells will be covered in thick, rubbery jackets. To see them shucked of their skins and in all their glory, drive 1km (½ miles) up H4021 to the **Phuket Shell Museum**, on the left nearly opposite the entrance to the Phuket Island Resort.

Displayed are tropical shells like Key Scallops, Nautilus, Variegated Sundials, the delicate spine-like Venus Comb Murexes, Turbans, Humpback Coweries, Olives and Cones. The shop sells many of them at reasonable prices.

For lunch or dinner, dine on seafood at the **Gan Eng 1** open-air seaside restaurant. Return to the Chalong intersection, turn right and follow the 1-km (½-mile) road to the sea. The restaurant, on the right, offers a large array of seafood dishes served under coconut palms. Your view is of Phuket's new yacht basin, but more interesting are the local boats which bear tail fins like those found on 1950's Chevrolets and Cadillacs.

19. Phuket Town

A walk through Phuket's history with Chinese temples, colonial mansions, and the heart of the former Chinese quarter.

Phuket's main market on **Ranong Road** holds all the sights, scents, and sounds of an eastern bazaar but it wakes up very early in the morning. Plan your visit to end before it winds down at 9am.

Exit the market, cross Ranong Road and walk to the left, passing the THAI **office**, housed in a beautiful old dwelling. Continue along Ranong past Wat Nua, a Thai Buddhist temple. At the next corner, cross to **Put Jaw Temple**. This 200-year-old Chinese Taoist temple, the oldest in Phuket, is dedicated to Kuan Im, Goddess of Mercy, whose image occupies the main hall.

On the floor before her are two cans of what looks like split bamboo chopsticks used to foretell the future. Shake the can until one of the sticks falls to the floor. Read the number. In the room on the left, in the pigeon-holed boxes on the right-hand wall, locate a slip of paper with the corresponding number. Get someone at your hotel to translate your fortune for you.

Roof detail, Put Jaw temple

Through a door in the left-hand compound wall is the more ornate Taoist **Jui Tui Temple**, dedicated to Kiu Wong In, the Vegetarian God. Of particular interest are the fine carvings of guardians on the huge teak doors. Many Vegetarian Festival activities take place here each September. In a building on the left are an ornate sedan chair and a chariot on which the image of the God is placed before it is pulled through the town's streets.

Exit Put Jaw, turn left and return to Ranong Road. Turn right again to Padiphat Road and right to Krabi Road. Cross the street and walk 50m (164ft) on the left to **Sanjao Sam San** which is set back from the road. Built in 1853, this shrine is dedicated to Tien Sang Sung Moo, the Goddess of the Sea and patron saint of sailors.

Continue down **Krabi Road**. On the left, spacious yards hold beautiful old colonial style houses built by late 19th-century rubber and tin barons. At the corner, turn left onto Satun (the sign says 'Satul') Road. At the next corner, turn right onto Deebuk Road

This colonial-style mansion houses the THAI office

(look out for another lovely colonial house on the opposite corner).

Walk down **Deebuk Road**. The Sino-Portuguese style rowhouses on the right are ancestral homes of old Chinese families. Look closely at the beautiful treatment of the entrances. Turn left on to **Yawaraj Road**. A short way up on the right is perhaps the most beautiful of the colonial houses, a two-storey residence with a yellow bargeboard. Just beyond, on the right, are more Sino-Portuguese shophouses and at the next traffic light is a colonial home in a pretty yard; another sits on the opposite corner.

Backtrack down Yawaraj and turn left onto Deebuk. Halfway down, turn right into **Soi Romanni** whose atmosphere evokes Phuket's Chinese past.

Soi Romanni exits onto Thalang Road. Turn right to the intersection with Yawaraj Road. On the opposite corner is a pretty colonial-style shop. Turn left on Yawaraj, walk to the traffic circle, turn right and within a few steps you arrive back at the market.

Head up Rang Hill for lunch at **Tung-ka Cafe**. This is one of the finest restaurants in Phuket for authentic Thai cuisine.

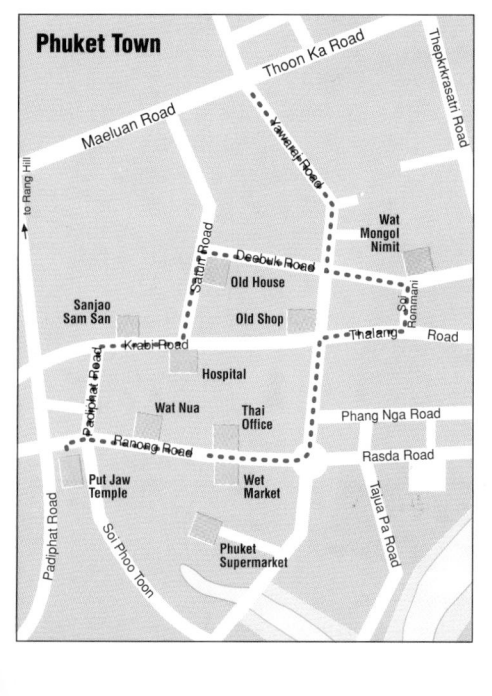

Phuket Town

Thoon Ka Road
Thepkkrasatri Road
Maeluan Road
Yawaraj Road
to Rang Hill
Satun Road
Deebuk Road
Wat Mongol Nimit
Old House
Soi Romanni
Sanjao Sam San
Old Shop
Thalang Road
Krabi Road
Padiphat Road
Hospital
Phang Nga Road
Wat Nua
Thai Office
Ranong Road
Rasda Road
Put Jaw Temple
Wet Market
Tajua Pa Road
Padiphat Road
Soi Phoo Toon
Phuket Supermarket

EXCURSIONS

20. Phang-nga from the South

A day-long boat trip takes you past mysterious monoliths and some of Asia's most spectacular scenery.

The stunning limestone monoliths of **Phang-nga Bay** (75km/46½ miles north-east of Phuket) which rise out of the water as in a Chinese brush painting, have long been a tourist favourite. Most visitors, however, enter it from the north. Try it from the south for a different perspective on a day-long excursion.

Some tour companies offer itineraries where guests sail into majestic Phang-nga Bay from Ao Po harbour in north-east Phuket. It is the most relaxing way to approach one of the most scenic areas of Southeast Asia. Try Jolly Roger (Tel: 340-800) and Siam Exclusive Tours (Tel: 340-912, 341-188). The sea journey is through a fantasy land of sheer-sided limestone plinths rising hundreds of metres out of the sea; in the early morning light, they are breathtaking.

The first stop is at **Koh Ping Kan**, first captured in the James Bond film *The Man With the Golden Gun*. Fronting it is the impressive **Koh Tapu** (Nail Island), a 40-metre (130-ft) tall finger of rock balanced on a very thin fingernail. Continue north through **Tham Lawd**, a natural tunnel running beneath a huge mountain. Stop at **Khao Khian** to look at cave drawings of ancient ships.

The lunch stop is at **Koh Pannyi**, a Muslim village built entirely on stilts. It once earned its living from fishing but now only fishes for tourists. However, it serves good Thai seafood lunches. Wander along its boardwalks to the mosque at the base of the tall limestone cliff.

On the return trip,

Monoliths rising from watery depths, Phang-nga

you can spend the afternoon swimming and sunning at **Naga Yai island**. Usually deserted, the beach offers a long, powdery sand foreshore and clear waters. The boat returns to Ao Po at 4.30pm.

21. Sea Canoeing in Phang-nga Caves

Voyage on a canoe into sea caves and lagoons in Phang-nga Bay. Pick a day trip, or three- and seven-day excursions.

Sea canoeing is an eco-friendly way to explore the wonders of **Phang-nga Bay**. Holding two passengers and a paddler, the kayaks are manoeuvred into caves and tunnels under huge limestone mountains rising from the bay.

Many of these monoliths are doughnut-shaped, hollow in the centre and open to the sky. The paddler times his entry to coincide

with ebbing tides to squeeze through narrow passages 40m (131ft) long. You emerge into a silent lagoon with mangroves and cliff-clinging trees inhabited by kingfishers and families of monkeys stranded there when the seas rose eons ago.

A day-trip begins with a hotel pick-up. A cruiser leaves Ao Po for an hour's

Manoeuvring through mangroves

trip into the heart of the bay where you can explore a number of caves. After lunch, you have the afternoon free to paddle on your own explorations or to relax on a deserted beach. This trip will set you back about 2,500 baht.

Also offered are overnight, three-day, and seven-day expeditions, as well as self-paddling trips to explore Phuket's coastline. Contact **Sea Canoe Thailand** at 367/3 Yaowaraj Road (on the left, about 1km past Vajira Hospital) at Tel: 212-172, 212-252.

22. Cruise to Phi Phi

A day cruise to the island jewels of Phi Phi to swim and snorkel. For those who wish to linger a day or two, there are island accommodations to suit all budgets.

Phi Phi (pronounced Pee Pee, not Fifi) islands are among the most beautiful in the world. While over development threatens to mar their pristine beauty, the sight of the palm-fringed limestone haystacks still make any traveller's heart leap.

The islands sit at the southern end of the Phang-nga chain 30½km (19½ miles) south-east of Phuket. The larger of the two, **Phi Phi Don**, 20km (12½ miles) in circumference, comprises two enormous mountains – one 498m (1,600ft) tall – linked by a narrow strip of sand to create what from the air would look like a giant high-backed chair. The strand is so narrow, you might think it possible to heave a rock across to the opposite shore. Nine coves of powdery sand, adjoining coral reefs, and warm, aquamarine waters give the island its reputation for unsurpassed beauty.

Just offshore is **Phi Phi Le**. It is more dramatic than Phi Phi Don and is famed for the birds which build nests prized by Chinese gourmets for bird's nest soup. Its caves hold prehistoric drawings of what appear to be Viking ships.

Ton Sai, Phi Phi Don's main tourist beach, is a two-hour boat ride from Ao Makham on Phuket island. A one-day tour from Ao Makham takes you to Phi Phi Don for lunch, then on to Phi Phi Le for a look at the bird nest collection area and the Viking Caves.

If you have a few days to spare, spend them on Phi Phi Don. Songserm Tours' (Tel: 222-570/4) round-trip day ticket can be broken into two days. Stay longer if you like but tell the agency first; the Songserm boat departs Ton Sai at 3pm daily.

Ton Sai beach holds the upmarket bungalows, shops, and restaurants. The southern beaches have bungalows for budget travellers. Reach them on foot or by long-tail boat taxis that leave from Ton Sai dock. My main reason for visiting Phi Phi Don is the grand vistas of island and sea one gets from a large flat rock located high on a bluff at the southern end of the island. To reach it, walk over the rocky headland at the south end of Ton Sai beach. Just past the bridge is an arrow to the left. Follow it and walk 45 minutes up a steep hill. Be sure to take a bottle of water with you on a hot day.

At the top, slump down on the rock, breathe deeply and drink in one of the most beautiful panoramas imaginable. Beyond the jungle canopy are the twin bays of Phi Phi barely separated by a thin strip of land. Behind them, an imposing Gibraltar of a mountain serves as a backdrop.

The twin bays of Phi Phi

Shopping

Thailand is one huge emporium of art and craft products. While each region has its own specialities, goods from all regions are available in Bangkok, Chiang Mai, and Phuket. You find the widest selection of goods and the best prices in Bangkok and Chiang Mai. Pay street vendors in cash; shops will accept cash or credit cards but expect a 3–5 percent surcharge for their use. Shops can arrange packing, shipping, and documentation at reasonable prices.

A warning: Thailand has been experiencing problems with unscrupulous jewellers who promise the sky (with certificates of authenticity) for fake or overvalued gems and jewellery. If someone suggests you can make a large profit by re-selling the gems in your own country, don't even think about it. Run. Also, avoid friendly street touts who strike up a conversation and offer to escort you to their friend's shop. You are being set up for a rip-off. Reputable shopowners do not operate this way.

Carved doorway

What to Buy

Antiques

A range of wood, bronze, terracotta, and stone statues from all regions of Thailand. You will also find carved wooden angels, mythical animals, temple bargeboards and eaves brackets. Although the Thai government prohibits the export of Buddha images, there are numerous other deities and disciples which can be sent abroad.

Neo-antiques

With genuine antiques in increasingly short supply, Thailand's artisans now create good copies. There is no attempt to sell them as antique items and the craftsmanship is quite remarkable. Buddha images, animals, precocious children, betelnut boxes and others in a variety of finishes are very popular.

Baskets

Thailand's abundant wicker and grasses are transformed into lamps, storage boxes, tables, colourful mats, handbags, letter holders, tissue boxes and slippers. Wicker and bamboo are turned into storage lockers and furniture; shops can provide the cushions. *Yan lipao*, a sturdy grass about the thickness of a broomstraw, is woven into delicately-patterned purses and bags for formal occasions.

Ceramics

Most Thai ceramic items come from the North. Best known is celadon, the jade-green, brown, or cobalt statues, lamps, ashtrays and other items marked by their finely glazed surfaces. Potters make blue-and-white porcelain pots, lamp bases, household items and figurines. Earthenware embraces pots, planters, and dinner sets in a rainbow of hues and designs. Also popular are the brown-glazed Shanghai jars bearing yellow dragons which the Thais fill with bath water and which are perfect as pots for plants. *Bencharong* (five colour) is a 16th-century Chinese treatment used on porcelain bowls, containers, and fine chinaware.

Laquerware

Comes in two varieties: gleaming gold and black, and matte red with black and/or green details. Items include ornate containers and trays, wooden figurines, woven bamboo baskets and Burmese-style Buddhist manuscripts.

Fabrics

Shimmering Thai silk is synonymous with Thailand. It is sold in a wide variety of colours; its hallmark being the tiny nubs which rise from its surface. The thick cloth is suitable for clothes and scarves, and home decor items including pillows, purses, and picture frames. *Mudmee* is a somber-hued, Northeastern tie-dye silk sold in lengths or as finished clothes. A centre for batik, the south offers both ready-made clothes and paintings.

Gems and Jewellery

An important source of rubies and sapphires, Thailand is now regarded as a world leader in cutting coloured gemstones and diamonds. Thai artisans set the stones in gold and silver jewellery in ethnic Thai and international designs. Burmese

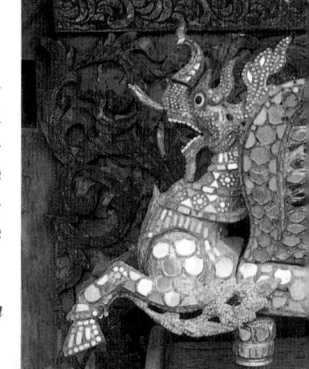

Mirrored mosaic dragon

jade is carved into jewellery and art objects. Pearl farms in Phuket create quality cultured pearls and pearl jewellery. Shop only at reputable stores. There are so many instances of tourists being sold fake goods that major shopowners have placed signs along Silom Road warning of rip-offs.

Hilltribe Crafts

Meo (Hmong), Mien (Yao), Lisu, Lahu, Akha and Karen tribes produce a wide selection of brightly-coloured needlepoint work in geometric and floral patterns which are used to decorate shirts, coats, bags and other personal items.

Although low in silver content, hilltribe silver is valued for its intricate craftsmanship and imaginatively-designed ceremonial necklaces, headdresses, bracelets and rings. Other hilltribe items include knives, baskets, pipes and a gourd flute that looks and sounds like a Scottish bagpipe.

Home Decor Items

Thailand's artificial flowers and fruits made of organza, poplin rayons, cotton, velvet, satin acetate, plastic, polyester and paper are virtually indistinguishable from fresh varieties. Burmese *kalaga* wall hangings depict gods, kings and mythical animals. The figures are stuffed with *kapok* to create a bas-relief effect. Papier mâché animals, boxes, vases and screens are superb gift and home decor items.

Furniture

Wooden furniture can include cabinets, tables, dining room sets, bedroom sets and kitchen utensils. It comes in natural hues or in whitewashed finishes and pastel colours.

Leather

Shoes, bags, wallets and belts are ordinary enough but the animals who contribute their hides are the oddest assortment – snake, armadillo, crocodile, lizard, frog, cow hide and even chicken.

Metal Art Objects

Bronze deities, characters from the *Ramakhien*, deer and abstract figures are cast up to 2m (6.6ft) tall and clad in gleaming brass skins. Bronze is also crafted into cutlery sets. Silver and gold are pounded into jewellery items, boxes and other decorative pieces, and set with gems. For neilloware boxes and receptacles, a design is incised in silver or gold. The background is cut away and filled with an amalgam of dark metals leaving the figures to stand in high relief. Phuket tin is the prime ingredient in pewterware clocks, steins, egg cups, and figurines.

Umbrellas

Perhaps Chiang Mai's most famous product, umbrellas made from silk and *sah koi* paper are hand-painted with nature motifs.

Where to Buy

Bangkok

This is the country's main marketplace for handicraft items. Look in the huge air-conditioned malls like **Amarin Plaza**, **Siam Centre**, **Mahboonkrong**, **Oriental Plaza**, and **Central Plaza**, or in major department stores. **River City complex** contains dozens of antique shops. Queen Sirikit's **Chitrlada** stores sell the rare crafts she and her organization, SUPPORT, have worked so diligently to preserve. There are branches in the airport, Grand Palace, Hilton Hotel and Pattaya. The Thai government's handicraft centre, **Narayana Phand**, at 127 Rajdamri Road, sells a wide array of Thai handicrafts. **New Road**, **Silom**, **Suriwong** and **Sukhumvit** are lined with crafts shops. **Sampeng Lane**, the **Thieves Market**, the Buddha amulet markets at **Tha Prajan** and **Wat Rajanadda** and the **Chatuchak Weekend Market** draw adventurous shoppers. Street vendors on the lower end of Sukhumvit Road, the lanes of **Siam Square**, **upper Silom Road**, **Rajdamri Avenue** and **Patpong Road**, sell souvenirs and cheap clothes.

Pewterware

Chiang Mai

In Chiang Mai, Borsang Road shops specialise in particular crafts (see Itinerary 9, *Chiang Mai* for details). Supported by His Majesty King Bhumibol, the Hilltribe Products Foundation operates **Border Crafts of Thailand**, at 21/17 Suthep Road, Wat Suan Dok (Tel: 277-743). Its branch, **Hill-Tribe Products Foundation**, is at 100/61–62 Huay Kaew Road near Chiang Mai University (Tel: 212-978).

Phuket

Phuket's beachside shops sell all manner of leisure wear but for handicrafts, try these shops along the main Airport-Phuket highway: **Thai Village**, 1km off H402 at KM2.5; **Native Handicraft Centre** on H402 at KM8.5; **Silk Master Handicrafts** on H402 at KM9; and **Thai Style**, at KM9. For seashells and shell products, visit **Phuket Seashell Co**, at KM8.5 on H402, 1km before Rawai.

An oversized silk fan

EATING OUT

Anyone who has tried Thai cuisine knows that it is one of the best in the world. Now, sample it in its home kitchens. For homesick palates, the country's foreign restaurants are also among the finest and least expensive in Asia.

It is a fallacy that all Thai cuisine is extremely spicy. In truth, many Thais cannot stand hot food. Chefs realise this and can bland any dish on request. Among the fiery favourites are *thom yam gung* (piquant soup with shrimp), *gaeng khiew wan gai* (a hot green curry with chicken or beef), and *gaeng phet* (a red curry with beef).

Among the non-spicy dishes are: *thom kha gai* (coconut milk curry with chicken), *plaamuk thawd krathiem prik Thai* (squid fried with garlic and black pepper; also with fish), *nua phat namman hoi* (beef in oyster sauce), *muu phat priew wan* (sweet and sour pork), and *hormok talay* (a fish or seafood mousse); which can be spiced up if you desire. Thais also make luscious sweets from coconut milk, tapioca and fruits. Some of the best are sold by sidewalk vendors. A plate of fresh Thai fruit is a delicious dessert. Try ice cream *kathit*, made of coconut milk.

Thai dishes are eaten with steamed white rice. Ladle a spoonful or two of a curry onto the rice and eat it before sampling the next curry so you do not obscure the unique flavour of each. The practical Thais eat with a fork in the left hand and spoon in the right, using the

Thai cuisine isn't always hot

fork to shovel the food onto the spoon and into the mouth.

The restaurants on the following pages are recommended as much for their atmosphere as for their superb food. Most restaurants close at 10pm; most hotel coffeeshops at midnight. You can probably be seated without a reservation but to be sure, telephone beforehand. A general guide to prices for a dinner for one excluding beverage, tax and tips are: Inexpensive = under 250 baht; Moderate = 250–350 baht; Expensive = over 350 baht.

Bangkok

Thai

BUSSARACUM
35 Soi Pipat 2, Convent Road
Tel: 235-8915
A homely atmosphere with live *jakae* Thai stringed music and some of the best Thai food in town. Their appetizers can be a meal by itself. *Moderate*

WHOLE EARTH
93/3 Soi Langsuan, Ploenchit
Tel: 252-5574
Elegant restaurant with classic Thai dining which appeals to a younger crowd. Option of sitting cross-legged on cushions at low tables. Convenient location for Soi Sarasin music bars. *Moderate*

LEMONGRASS
5/1 Soi 24, Sukhumvit Road
Tel: 258-8637
Superb Thai food using traditional Thai recipes and served in an old Thai home. Popular with Thais (the ultimate test). Reservations necessary. *Moderate*

SALA RIM NAAM
Opposite The Oriental Hotel
Tel: 437-6211
Ride the Oriental Hotel's ferry to this Thai-style, riverside restaurant. A cultural programme and well-prepared cuisine. *Expensive*

A Thai breakfast

TASSANEYA NAVA
Book at World Travel Service at the Oriental Hotel
Tel: 236-0420
A converted rice barge cruises up and down the Chao Phya River, serving a set meal of Thai cuisine. A great way to dine and see the nighttime shoreline. *Expensive*

TUMNAK THAI
131 Ratchadapisek Road
Tel: 277-3828, 277-8855
This is the world's largest restaurant and serves a variety of Thai regional dishes in a village setting. *Moderate*

Chinese

SILVER PALACE RESTAURANT
5 Soi Pipat, Silom Road
Tel: 235-5118
Chiu Chao (southern Chinese) cuisine at its best in a brightly-lit setting. *Moderate*

Indian

HIMALI CHA CHA
1229/11 New Road
Tel: 235-1569
Northern Indian cuisine served in an intimate atmosphere. Menu created by the late Cha Cha, one of Lord Mountbatten's former chefs. *Moderate*

Indonesian

BALI
15/3 Soi Ruam Rudee
Ploenchit Road
Tel: 254-3581
Indonesian cuisine served in a cosy dining room. To sample a range of curries, order Rijistafel. *Moderate*

Vietnamese

LE DALAT
51 Soi 23, Sukhumvit Road
Tel: 258-4192
Imperial Vietnamese cuisine in a refined setting. *Moderate*

Japanese

HANAYA
683 Siphya Road
Tel: 234-8095
Choice favourites like an excellent *nigiri sushi*. *Moderate*

French

LE BISTROT
20/18–19 Ruam Rudee Village
Soi Ruam Rudee, Ploenchit Road
Tel: 252-9651
Fine French dining in a quiet ambience. A wide selection of fine wines as well. *Expensive*

German

BEI OTTO
No 18, Soi 20, Sukhumvit Road
Tel: 258-1496
Sturdy German fare in a convivial atmosphere. Favoured by the German community. *Inexpensive*

British

ANGUS STEAK HOUSE
9/4–5 Thaniya Road
Tel: 234-3590
Grilled imported steaks are the speciality. Has been a favourite for a decade or more. *Moderate*

Italian

L'OPERA
55 Soi 39, Sukhumvit Road
Tel: 258-5605
Northern Italian cuisine and a good selection of wines in a softly-lit atmosphere. *Moderate*

American

BOURBON ST
Off Soi 22, Sukhumvit Road
(behind Washington Theatre)
Tel: 259-0328
Cajun specialities in this sports bar where expatriates gather to talk, or watch live or recorded ESPN sports. *Inexpensive*

Chiang Mai

Thai

THE GALLERY
25–29 Charoenrat Road
Tel: 248-601/2
Superb Thai cuisine in an old house and garden on the river. A must. *Moderate*

OLD CHIANG MAI CULTURAL CENTRE
185/3 Wua Lai Road
Tel: 274-093
Typical northern *khantoke* dinner with cultural programme of dance and music. *Moderate*

RIVERSIDE RESTAURANT
9–11 Charoenrat Road
(just opposite the Chinda Hospital)
Tel: 243-239
Noisy but lively with live music and good Thai and European fare overlooking the river. *Inexpensive*

English

THE PUB
Huay Kaew Road
(near the Rincome Hotel)
Tel: 211-550
A standby for decades. A house in a quiet garden with excellent English fare. *Inexpensive*

French

LE COQ D'OR
68/1 Koh Klan Road, Nong Hoi
Tel: 282-024
Refined dining in an old house. Not easy to reach but worth trying. *Moderate*

German

HAUS MUNCHEN
115/3 Loi Kroa Road

Tel: 274-027
Located opposite Suriwongse Hotel, this is a long-established hostelry with draft beer, German *schnaps* and homemade breads. *Moderate*

Italian
PENSIONE LA VILLA
145 Rajdamnern Road
Tel: 277-403
Good standard fare at reasonable prices. *Inexpensive*

Japanese
MUSASHI
53/6 Inthawarot Road
Tel: 210-944
A favourite with Japanese visitors. *Inexpensive*

Phuket

Phuket Town
TUNK-KA CAFE
Rang Hill
Tel: 212-040
A long hike up Phuket's tallest hill to a garden view over the city and some excellent southern Thai food. Try *kung siap* shrimp. *Inexpensive*

Patong
BAAN RIM PA
190/7 Kalim Beach Road
Tel: 340-789
Probably Phuket's best Thai restaurant. Elegant with clifftop view. Must reserve. *Moderate*

MALEE SEAFOOD VILLAGE
Thaweewong (Beach) Road
50 metres south of Soi Bangla
Tel: 340-205
Busy outdoor seafood emporium in central Patong. Choose fish, prawns, oysters, crab and lobster from the mouth-watering iceboat display. Priced by weight. *Moderate*

TUM & No. 4
82 Soi Bangla
Two informal and acclaimed seafood restaurants side by side. In the heart of the nightlife area. *Inexpensive*

PIZZERIA NAPOLI
Soi Patong Post Office
Tel: 340-674
Indoor dining on a wide range of Italian specialities. *Inexpensive*

SHALIMAR
89/59 Soi Patong Post Office
Tel: 340-644
Food from the sub-continent amidst a charming Indian atmosphere. *Inexpensive*

Rustic beachside dining

Karon
ON THE ROCK
Marina Cottages
Tel: 330-625, 330-493/7
As the name suggests, this restaurant is perched on a cliffside, overlooking Karon Bay. Serves superb Thai and European seafood dishes. *Moderate*

Kata
BOATHOUSE WINE AND GRILL
Boathouse Inn
Tel: 330-557/8
Award-winning reštaurant serving superb Thai and western food on a terrace overlooking the beach. Extensive wine list and set menus available. *Moderate*

Nightlife

Bangkok

If the world knows nothing else about Thailand, it knows about its vibrant nightlife. There is little of cultural interest but plenty of entertainment outlets that include discos, jazz clubs, trendy bistros, and a bar scene that is renowned throughout the world. Whatever one chooses, one will eventually gravitate to the throbbing nightlife nerve centres of the city. Here is a sample of what is available:

Go-Go Bars

Bars with hostesses are concentrated in the **Nana Plaza** (Soi 4, Sukhumvit Road), **Soi Cowboy** (between Sois 21 and 23, Sukhumvit) and **Patpong** (between Silom and Suriwong roads). The first two are a bit seedy, so that leaves Patpong. Patpong is not one but three short streets, the first two devoted to go-go bars and Patpong 3 catering to the gay community. On Patpong 1, **King's Castle** is typical. Bikinied go-go girls dance on a platform while others wander around the room, ready to sit with men willing to buy them drinks. The girls can be taken out for other nocturnal activities, but if it is before the bar closes (2am), the customer must pay the bar a fee. Other negotiations are entirely between the girl and the customer, but be forewarned that it is a seller's market. With AIDS on the rise, do not be foolish; the pharmacy is just down the street.

Live Shows

The shows at **Pink Panther, Firecat, Look**, and **Pussy Galore** are more titillating than erotic. Beware of the live sex shows off Patpong or along Patpong 2 (the kind the touts want to steer you to). Imbibers may find themselves being handed extortionate

Sundown scene

bills of 2,000-plus baht by very large bouncers. If this should happen to you, hand over the money and try to get a copy of the bill. Head straight for the police booth on the Suriwong Road end of Patpong 2 or to the Tourist Police at the intersection of Silom and Rama 4 roads. The police do not tolerate this kind of thuggery and if you act quickly, you can often get your money back.

Barbeers

In the open-air 'barbeers' along **Patpong 2**, the primary activity is watching video movies and the passing scene, and chatting. **Soi Cowboy** used to be regarded as Patpong's poor relative but in recent years a number of its bars have become quite respectable. The street of bars runs between **Sois 21** and **23** just north of Sukhumvit Road. **Nana Entertainment Complex** is a mélange of barbeers, restaurants, and nightclubs on two floors of a shopping complex 80m (260ft) inside Soi 4, Sukhumvit.

Massage Parlours

The emphasis is upon total relaxation, but not achieved in a manner mum would approve. You pick a girl from behind a glass partition and then spend the next hour getting a bath and whatever else you arrange with her. In B-course massages, the girl uses her naked body to massage yours. Again, take prophylactic precautions should things get out of hand.

Pubs

Nice enough to take a date are the pubs along **Sukhumvit, Soi 33**. Most waitresses speak English. For an evening of good fun and music, try the nightclubs along **Soi Sarasin** and **Soi Lang Suan**, and **Sukhumvit Soi 55**. The emphasis is on good live music and they appeal as much to young professional Thais as they do to Westerners.

Jazz Clubs

Among the most popular is **Brown Sugar** (Soi Sarasin) and **Round Midnight** (Soi Lang Suan); the latter offers jazz on Monday and Saturday nights. **Saxophone** at the Victory Monument (3/8 Phya Thai Road) plays jazz standards. Local residents gather Sunday evenings at 8pm at **Bobby's Arms** to play excellent Dixieland jazz. The club is located on the first floor of the carpark above Foodland on Patpong 2 Road. **Witch's Tavern** offers jazz and English roasts on Sukhumvit 55, opposite Soi 9. **Boulevard Hotel** presents jazz on Sunday afternoons from 2pm. Oriental Hotel's **Bamboo Bar** is for dressier occasions with jazz singers from the US performing nightly.

Discos

Peppermint Bistro on Patpong Road is packed after 11pm. **Bubbles** in the Dusit Thani Hotel is a perennial favourite. The chic **Rome Club** gay videotheque on Patpong 3, open till 3am, is often packed with dancers of all persuasions.

Chiang Mai

Music Bars

By comparison with Bangkok, Chiang Mai's nightlife is casual and subdued. The most popular places are the music bars along both sides of the moat near Tapae Gate. Among the most popular are **Old West** on Huay Kaew Road, and **Early Times** and **Captain Hook's** on Kotchasan Road. **Baritone** at 96 Post office Road presents jazz nightly at 9pm. Bars with hostesses, like **Blue Moon** at 5/3 Moon Muang Road and **Spotlight** at 47 Kochasan Road, are quiet drinking places without the ubiquitous go-go girls found elsewhere in Thailand.

Gay Bars

The **Butterfly Room** at 126 Loi Khroa Road and the **Coffee Boy** at 248 Toonghotel Road are popular.

Discos

The Plaza, Chiang Mai Plaza Hotel; **The Wall**, Chiang Inn Hotel.

Phuket

Barbeers

Phuket puts its balmy night air to good use with a wealth of open-air bars. They tend to be loud and the action raucous with the primary entertainment comprising watching videos, conversing with hostesses and people-watching. Most nightlife is concentrated in Patong Beach's **Soi Bangla**, with the two biggest concentrations behind **Baby Bar** and **Gonzo Cafe**. Look also along **Soi Sunset City** and its two adjacent sois to the east of Soi Bangla. Barbeers have also sprung up on **Karon** and **Kata** beaches.

Barbeer scene, Patong

Discos

Titanic, Soi Sunset City next to Expat Hotel; and **Banana Disco** at 94 Thaviwong Road next to the Patong Beach Hotel.

Pubs

For a quiet atmosphere try **Paradise Bar** on Thaviwong Road next to Holiday Inn. **English Pub** on Soi Patong Resort off Soi Bangla has a pool table.

Gay Bars

A large number of gay bars and meeting places are concentrated in the **Paradise Complex** in front of the **Royal Paradise Hotel** off Rat-Uthit Road in Patong.

Calendar of Special Events

Plan your visit to coincide with a Thai festival. Thais celebrate even their religious holidays with gusto and invite the visitor to join in. Check with the Tourism Authority of Thailand (TAT) for exact dates as these may vary from year to year.

January

Borsang Umbrella Fair (Chiang Mai): Mid-month. This colourful festival honours the craftsmen who make Chiang Mai's beautiful umbrellas. Parades, cultural presentations, and craft demonstrations are held.

February

Flower Festival (Chiang Mai): Early-February. This is the period when flowers are abloom in the cool air. Flower exhibitions are staged but the key event is a grand floral procession through the streets of the city, with floats, marching bands and beautiful Chiang Mai women.

Magha Puja (Nationwide): Full moon night. Celebrates the gathering of 1,200 disciples to hear Buddha preach. As the full moon rises, buy incense sticks, a candle and flowers, and join a candlelight procession around a Buddhist temple. After completing three circuits, place your candle, incense sticks and flowers in the sand-filled trays, *wai* (hands clasped in prayer before the face) and depart.

Kite flying season (Bangkok): At Sanam Luang, next to Wat Phra Kaew, kids fly kites of every shape and colour while older Thais compete in ancient kite battles. The season runs through April.

April

Songkran (Nationwide): 13–15 April. The traditional Thai new year when one blesses friends by sprinkling water on them. It quickly develops into a fun, full-scale war with ample dousings. Expect to get drenched and dress appropriately. Chiang Mai (along the banks of the Ping River) and the small towns have the rowdiest action.

May

Loy Rua (Sea Gypsy festival, Phuket): Full moon days. Fisherman set adrift bamboo boats on the sea to carry away bad luck.

Visakha Puja (Nationwide): Full moon night. Commemorates Buddha's birth, enlightenment and death, which all occurred on the same day. It is celebrated in the same manner as Magha Puja.

The Plowing Ceremony (Bangkok): Mid-month. An ancient, brilliantly-colourful ceremony presided over by King Bhumibol and marking the beginning of the rice season. At Sanam Luang. Buy tickets at the TAT office.

July

Asalaha Puja (Nationwide): Full moon night. Commemorates Buddha's first sermon to his first five disciples. It is celebrated in the same manner as Magha Puja.

September

Chinese Moon Festival (Nationwide): Full moon night of the eighth lunar month. It is a lovely festival where lanterns and shrines are alight to honour the Moon Goddess. Sample the scrumptious moon cakes which are found at no other time of the year.

International Swan Boat Races (Bangkok): Held under Bangkok's Rama 9 Bridge. Draws participants from all around the world.

Vegetarian Festival (Phuket): Mid-month, but sometimes in October. The most unusual of Phuket's festivals. There are daily street processions but its most salient features are tests of devotion that are not for the squeamish. Devotees enter trances and perform feats of daring including climbing ladders with rungs made of knives, running skewers, hoses, spears, even Chiang Mai umbrellas through

cheeks and tongues, and the most daring feat – walking barefoot across fiery coals. To enter the temples, dress entirely in white.

October

Chonburi Buffalo Races (Chonburi Province): Water buffaloes and their farmboy jockeys race for prizes.

November

Loy Krathong (Nationwide): Full moon night. The most beautiful of Thai celebrations. Thais (and foreigners) launch tiny candle-bearing boats in streams and ponds to wash away sins and bless love affairs. It is a romantic night for lovers of all ages.

Loy Krathong offerings

December

Trooping of the Colours (Bangkok): 3 December. Two days before his birthday, His Majesty reviews his colourful regiments at the Rama V Plaza. Get tickets at TAT offices.

Phuket King's Cup Regatta (Phuket): Early December. A long-distance yacht race which has become a fixture on international yachting calendars. Centred at Nai Harn beach.

Chiang Mai Winter Fair (Chiang Mai): Late December. The annual winter fair offers cultural shows, the Miss Chiang Mai contest and a product fair at the Municipal Stadium.

Practical Information

GETTING THERE

By Air

More than 40 airlines serve Bangkok. Chiang Mai and Phuket can be reached from Bangkok on the domestic arm of Thai Airways International (THAI). Dragonair, Lauda Air, and Silkair now fly directly to Phuket from Vienna, Sydney, Singapore and Hong Kong. A 200 baht tax for international flights is charged at the airport on departure.

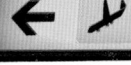

ผู้โดยสารขาเข้า ลายต่างประเทศ
INTERNATIONAL ARRIVAL

From the Airport

Bangkok: The journey from the airport into town takes 45–120 minutes depending on traffic. There are three taxi services: THAI air-conditioned limousines (300 baht); luxury cars (400 baht); and THAI air-conditioned mini-vans (100 baht) which leave the airport every 30 minutes.

Airport Taxi, a private limousine operator, offers service to city hotels and homes for about the same price.

Ordinary air-conditioned taxis are the cheapest alternative. Buy a ticket at the desk on the southern end of the terminal, and on arrival at your destination, pay the driver the amount stated on it.

If transferring directly to a domestic flight, take the free shuttle bus which runs at 15-minute intervals to the Domestic Terminal.

Chiang Mai: The airport is a 10-minute drive from the city centre. Major hotel vans ferry guests to their doors (50 baht). You can make a reservation at the airport. A THAI mini-van runs between the airport and its office at 240 Phrapoklao Road (20 baht). You must find your own way from the office to your hotel.

Phuket: The airport is on the northern end of the island, a 30-km (45-minute) drive from Phuket town. Major hotels provide limousines but charge up to 500 baht per car.

THAI Ground Services offers air-conditioned limousines to each beach for 250–450 baht per car. THAI mini-vans run between the airport and its Phuket town office on Ranong Road (70 baht), and to Patong, Kata, or Karon beaches (100 baht).

TRAVEL ESSENTIALS

When to Visit

While Thailand is tropical, ie hot and humid, there are regional variations in temperature. Seasons are divided into Hot (mid-February to late May), Rainy (June to mid-November); and Cool (mid-November to mid-February). The cool season is the best but the monsoon season can also be pleasant, except for September when the rain falls incessantly. Avoid the Christmas, New Year and Chinese New Year (January/February) periods when hotels, especially in Phuket, tend to be full.

Visas & Passports

Thai embassies and consulates overseas issue 60-day Tourist Visas (300 baht) or 30-day Transit Visas (200 baht). Free 15-day Transit Visas are given on arrival at Bangkok, Chiang Mai, or Phuket airports to most nationalities. All visas can be extended for a nominal fee at Immigration offices.

Vaccinations

Although the chance of contracting them is virtually nil, polio, rabies, Japanese encephalitis, and typhoid fever vaccinations are recommended for a visit to Thailand. Persons arriving from a Yellow Fever area must carry a certificate attesting to recent inoculation.

Customs

Thailand bans firearms, pornographic materials, and drugs. Cash imports of over $10,000 must be declared. The Bangkok Airport has a green and red Customs channel and any searches are brief and polite.

IMMIGRATION

Weather

In Bangkok the seasons are as follows:

Hot: March to mid-June, 27–35°C (80–95°F).

Rainy: June to October, 24–32°C (75–90°F).

Cool: November to February, 18–32°C (65–90°F), but lower humidity.

Chiang Mai enjoys a cooler climate. In the cool season, temperatures range between 13 and 28°C (55 and 82°F) and lower in the hills. Like Bangkok, the heaviest rain falls in September and city streets often flood.

In **Phuket**, the monsoon begins early May but generally ends late in October. Temperatures range from 34°C (93°F) in the hot season to nighttime temperatures of 21°C (70°F) in the cool season. The water temperature never drops below 20°C (68°F).

Clothing

Clothes should be light and loose; natural fibres or blends are preferable to synthetics because they can 'breathe' in the humid air. Sunglasses are essential; light hats protect heads on sunny days. Shorts are taboo for men and women at temples and mosques. Shoes must be removed upon entering temple buildings, so slip-on shoes (not sandals) are best.

Northern winter nights can be quite chilly; hill trekking can be even colder. A sweater is welcome in the evenings or when travelling by motorcycle.

Electricity

Electrical outlets are rated at 220 volts, 50 cycles, and accept flat-pronged plugs.

Time Differences

Thailand is seven hours ahead of Greenwich Mean Time (GMT).

GETTING ACQUAINTED

Geography

At 514,000sq km (198,455sq miles), Thailand is approximately the size of France but has a population of 58 million people. Nearly 80 percent of its population grow rice, maize, sugar, tapioca, rubber, and a wide variety of fruits and vegetables. It also catches and cans fish and shellfish and is the world's third largest producer of tin.

Bangkok, the nation's capital, is divided by the Chao Phya River into twin cities – Bangkok and Thonburi – governed by the same municipality. Situated at 14 degrees north latitude, its 1,565sq km (604sq miles) area holds some eight million people.

Thailand's second largest city, **Chiang Mai**, lies 696km (432½ miles) north of Bangkok, in hills dominated by the country's highest mountain, Doi Inthanond, at 2,595m (8,514ft) tall. Chiang Mai sits 313m (1,027ft) above sea level, and is crowned by Doi Suthep, which rises to a height of 1,073m (3,521ft). The city is home to 120,000 people.

Phuket, an island in the Andaman Sea, lies 890km (553 miles) or a 70-minute flight south of Bangkok. Measuring 48.7km (30 miles) long by 21.3km (13 miles) wide, it is approximately the size of Singapore.

Government and Economy

Thailand is a constitutional monarchy with power vested in a freely-elected Parliament and a Senate appointed by His Majesty the King from ranking civilian and military officials. The executive branch comprises a coalition of political parties who select a Prime Minister who rules through a Cabinet. There is an independent judiciary.

Thailand enjoys a vigorous free-enterprise economy. Tourism is the principal money earner, followed by agricultural produce and commodities. In the late 1980s, it embarked on an ambitious programme of industrialization which has transformed the countryside and recorded annual GNP growth figures as high as 13 percent. It has a well-developed telecommunications, road and power infrastructure. But with the rapid growth, all these basic services are now under considerable pressure. Nonetheless, Thailand's economic development rates as one of the admirable success stories of Asia.

Religion

Ninety-two percent of the population profess their faith in Theravada Buddhism. Five percent are Muslims, most of whom inhabit the southern region. The rest of the population is Christian, Hindu, or Sikh. Hilltribes practice animism but many tribes, like the Karens and Lahu, have converted to Christianity.

How Not To Offend

The Royal Family is regarded with genuine reverence. Never make disparaging remarks about them and always stand when the Royal Anthem is played before the start of a movie.

Disrespect towards Buddha images, temples or monks is not taken lightly. Monks' vows of chastity prohibits them from touching women, even their mothers. When in the vicinity of a monk, a woman should keep her distance to avoid accidentally brushing against him.

Regardless of their religion, Thais take a dim view of men or women entering temples or mosques in shorts and sleeveless dresses.

Like many Asian cultures, Thais believe that the head is the fount of wisdom. It is therefore an insult to touch another person on the head, point one's foot at him, or step over him. Kicking in anger is worse than spitting on a Thai.

Whom Do You Trust?

Thailand is generally free of violent crime towards foreigners but you should be wary nonetheless: behind some Thai smiles lurks evil intent. With the increasing numbers of tourist arrivals, pickpockets and purse snatchers are on the rise in Bangkok. At major tourist attractions, beware of men and women offering free tours or directing you to shops offering special prices. At boat docks, avoid men offering you free rides on a canal boat; they'll take you for more than just a ride. Walk past bogus boy scouts with their notebooks soliciting donations. Above all, don't succumb to the lure of easy money by getting into a card game; it is rigged against your winning.

MONEY MATTERS

Currency

The Thai baht is divided into 100 satangs. Banknote denominations include 1,000 (gray), 500 (purple), 100 (red), 50 (blue), 20 (green) and 10 (brown) baht notes.

Ten-baht coins are brass discs encircled by a silver frame. Five-baht coins are silver with copper rims. There are three silver one-baht coins but only the small one will fit in a public telephone. There are two types of 50 and 25 satang coins.

The generally stable Thai currency was rated at 25 baht to the US dollar at press time. Most newspapers list daily rates.

Credit Cards

American Express, Diner's Club, Mastercard and Visa are widely accepted throughout Bangkok, Chiang Mai, Phuket and major up-country towns. Expect a surcharge of between 3 and 5 percent on their use at some outlets, especially American Express cards.

Cash Machines

Visas and Mastercards can be used to get cash advances at Bank of Ayutthaya, Thai Farmers Bank, Siam Commercial Bank and Thai Military Bank. Use the same cards for cash at ATMs at all the above banks except Bank of Ayutthaya. Obtain cash advances for American Express cards at Bangkok Bank. The main Chiang Mai and Phuket branches of these banks offer the same service.

Tipping

Higher-class restaurants add a service charge to the bill, but in ordinary restaurants, tip the waiter at least 10 percent and especially if you've been given good service. There is no tipping for noodle shops, street vendors, room boys, taxi or *tuk-tuk* drivers.

Taxes

There is 7 percent VAT charge on hotel room rates and on some restaurant items.

Money Changers

Hotels generally give poor rates, so change money at a bank. You will get better rates for travellers cheques than for cash. Banks are open from 8.30am to 3.30pm. Banks also operate exchange kiosks in major towns throughout Thailand. Open from 8.30am to 8pm.

GETTING AROUND

Domestic Air

Thai International domestic carrier flies to most major towns with around 10 flights a day to Chiang Mai and 11 to Phuket. The airport tax levied for domestic flights is 20 baht.

Rail

Thailand has an extensive domestic rail system serving most major cities. Overnight sleeper service is simple but comfortable and a preferable alternative to overnight buses whose safety record leaves something to be desired. For shorter journeys, the express Diesel Railcars are air-conditioned and comfortable.

The notable exception is the Bangkok-Chiang Mai service. Four comfortable sleeper trains run daily between Bangkok and Chiang Mai, leaving at 3, 6, 7.40 (Nakhon Ping Express) and 10pm. The journey takes 12–13 hours. Passenger seats fold down into comfortable beds. Either dine at your seat or walk along to the restaurant car. Waiters serve drinks throughout. Platform vendors hawk snacks through the train windows. Return trains leave Chiang Mai at 3.30, 4.40, 9.05 (Nakhon Ping Express) and 10.40pm. Choose from first and second class air-conditioned cars or second class fan-cooled cars.

A combination train-bus service runs between Bangkok and Phuket. The overnight train departs Bangkok in the evening, arriving at the southern town of Surat Thani in the morning. Passengers then transfer to a bus for the remaining five-hour drive to Phuket town.

For schedule details and reservations, visit Bangkok's **Hualampong Station** on Rama 4 Road. Many travel agents can also make train bookings.

Limousines

Major hotels in Bangkok and Chiang Mai and a few in Phuket have fleets of comfortable air-conditioned limousines. Prices are twice those of ordinary taxis, but they offer the convenience of English-speaking drivers, door-to-door service, and set fares.

Taxis

Bangkok taxis are reliable and air-conditioned, but the drivers' command of English is often less than perfect. Meter taxis now dominate. These are more com-

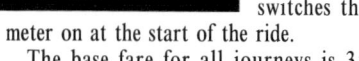

fortable yet cheaper than the old barter taxis. Just make sure the driver switches the meter on at the start of the ride.

The base fare for all journeys is 35 baht. There is no extra charge for baggage handling and stowage or for extra passengers. No tipping is required. There are no taxi stands; you stand on the curb and wave down a passing taxi. Avoid parked taxis as they usually ask more than those you flag down. There are no taxis in Chiang Mai or Phuket.

Tuk-tuks

Tuk-tuks (also called *samlors*) are the bright blue and yellow three-wheeled taxis whose name comes from the rattling noise their engines make. Most drivers do not speak English. Fares also begin at 30 baht.

In **Chiang Mai** and **Phuket**, the starting price is 20 baht. *Samlors*, the pedal

trishaws, charge 10 baht for short distances. Bargain before you board.

Motorcycle taxis

Reasonably safe ways to negotiate traffic during the rush hour in Bangkok (about 18 hours a day) are motorcycle taxis. There are stands at nearly every intersection; look for the boys wearing vests. The price must be bargained and can be close to that of taxis, but you are paying money in order to gain time. Helmets are now required; the drivers carry extra ones for their passengers.

In **Chiang Mai**, motorcycle taxis run up the Mae Sa Valley road from Mae

Rim to Mae Sa Falls, passing the elephant camp and orchid farms. In **Phuket**, motorcycle taxis leave from the market on Ranong Road.

Buses

Bangkok: Air-conditioned buses run more than a dozen routes through the city. Base fares for the blue and white buses start at 6 baht. Ordinary red and white (3.50 baht; 5 baht after 11pm) and blue and white (2.50 baht) buses operate more than 120 routes. The route numbers of air-conditioned buses do not correspond with those of ordinary buses.

Green mini-buses are smaller but their route numbers correspond to those of ordinary buses since they ply the same routes. They charge 2.50 baht; 4 baht after 10pm. Many bus lines halt service at midnight. Tourist maps give routes.

Chiang Mai: Yellow buses and red buses ply five routes and charge 2 to 4 baht depending on distance. Chiang Mai tourist maps note routes.

Phuket: Picturesque wooden buses leave every 30 minutes between 8am and 6pm from Phuket town market for all beaches. Buses to Rawai and Nai Harn, however, leave from the traffic circle on Bangkok Road. Flag one down. Fares are 10–25 baht. Minibuses run between Patong and Karon/Kata beaches for 20–40 baht. In Phuket town and Patong, they charge 10 baht per person regardless of distance travelled.

Rental Cars

In all three cities, Avis, Hertz and local agencies offer late model cars (Chiang Mai and Phuket rent 4WD jeeps) with or without drivers, inclusive of insurance coverage. First Class insurance with 2,000 baht deductible covers you and other vehicles involved in a collision. Expect to pay a 2,000 baht or more deposit, and a drop fee of 2,500 baht. An International Driver's License is valid in Thailand. Unlimited mileage; you pay for fuel.

In **Bangkok**, Avis, 2/12 Wireless Road, is open daily 8.30am to 5.30pm (Tel: 255-5300/4). Its desk at the Dusit Thani Hotel is open 24 hours a day (Tel: 238-0032). Hertz, at 420 Soi 71, Sukhumvit

Road (Tel: 390-0341, 390-1705, 391-0461) is open from 8am to 5pm.

In **Chiang Mai**, Avis at 14/14 Huay Kaew Road (Tel: 222-013, 221-316), at Royal Princess Hotel (Tel: 281-033/43) and at the airport (Tel: 222-013) are open 8am–6pm to rent sedans, vans and

jeeps. Hertz, at 12/3 Loi Kroa Road (Tel: 275-416, 279-473), Novotel Suriwongse (Tel: 270-051), and Chiang Mai Plaza (Tel: 270-040), rents the usual plus Mercedes Benzs and 12-passenger vans.

In **Phuket**, both Avis (Tel: 327-358) and Hertz (Tel: 327-463) are at the Airport and major hotels.

Motorcycle Rentals

Motorcycles are not advisable in Bangkok. Motorcycles in Chiang Mai and Phuket range from 90cc Honda Dreams to 125cc and 250cc trailbikes. Rental outlets can be found along beach roads and main roads in each town.

You must surrender your passport for the duration of the rental period, so change money first.

In **Chiang Mai**, Pop's is located at 51 Kotchasan Road, a short walk south of Tapae Gate (Tel: 274-014). If you pay a 2,000 baht deposit, Pop's will be content with a photocopy of your passport. You can find other rental companies along Chang Klan Road, Tapae Gate, and Chaiyaphum Road.

In **Phuket**, look along Rasda Road in Phuket town; Phuket Horizon Tour at 108/1 Rasda Road and Pure Car Rent (Tel: 211-002) opposite Thavorn Hotel. Patong MC Centre (the sign says 'Local Motion'), at the intersection of Soi Bangla and Rat-uthit (parallel the beach road), offers a wide selection.

For heavy bikes, see Patong Big Bike (62/1–2 Rat-uthit Road Tel: 340-380) just to the north of MC Centre.

HOURS & HOLIDAYS

Business Hours

Business hours are from 8 or 8.30am to 5.30pm, Monday through Friday. Some businesses are open Saturdays 8.30am–12pm. Government offices work from 8.30am–4.30pm, Monday–Friday.

Banking hours are from 8.30am–3.30pm, Monday–Friday, whilst bank-operated money-changing kiosks operate between 8.30am–8pm daily. Post office hours are 8.30am–4pm; an Indra Hotel branch opens until 8pm. The General Post Office on New Road between Suriwong and Siphya roads opens Monday–Friday, 8.30am–4.30pm; Saturday, 8.30am–12.30pm.

Department stores are open 10am–9pm, seven days a week. Shops, restaurants, and pharmacies open at 8.30 or 9am; most closing at 10pm.

Public Holidays

These days are observed as official public holidays:
New Year's Day: January 1
Magha Puja: February full moon
Chakri Day: April 6
Songkran: April 13
Labour Day: May 1
Coronation Day: May 5
Visakha Puja: May full moon
Asalaha Puja: July full moon
HM the Queen's Birthday: August 12
Chulalongkorn Day: October 23
HM the King's Birthday: December 5
Constitution Day: December 10
New Year's Eve: December 31

Chinese New Year in January/February (date determined by lunar calendar) is not officially recognised as a holiday, but many shops close for four days.

ACCOMMODATION

Bangkok

All hotels', except guesthouses, have shopping arcades, pool, restaurants, and air-conditioning. Add 7 percent VAT and a

10 percent service charge to rooms. You can bargain, especially during the low season (May–October).

Price categories (for a single room) are as follows: $ = under 1,000 baht; $$ = 1,000–1,999 baht; $$$ = 2,000–2,999 baht; $$$$ = 3,000–4,999 baht; $$$$$ = above 5,000 baht.

THE ORIENTAL
48 Oriental Avenue, New Road
Tel: 236-0400, 236-0420
The queen of Thailand's hotels is set in a garden on the river's edge. A good place to begin an exploration of the river. Excellent restaurants. *$$$$$*

THE REGENT OF BANGKOK
155 Rajdamri Road
Tel: 251-6127
Elegance in a city centre location, lovely atrium, first-class restaurants including the Spice Market, one of the best for Thai food. *$$$$$*

SHANGRI-LA
89 Soi Wat Suan Plu, New Road
Tel: 236-7777
A more formal riverside hotel with superb views from the upper floors. Their waterside Thai restaurant is excellent. *$$$$$*

ROYAL ORCHID SHERATON
Captain Bush Lane, Siphya Road
Tel: 234-5599
Another riverside hotel, this one with splendid views and easy access to China-town. *$$$$*

SUKHOTHAI
13/3 S. Sathorn Road
Tel: 287-0222
Bangkok's newest luxury hotel. Quiet, understated elegance. For those who want peace and quiet after a day on Bangkok's streets. *$$$$*

SIAM INTER-CONTINENTAL
Rama I Road
Tel: 253-0355/6
In the heart of the shopping district in a huge tropical garden. Good sports facilities. *$$$$*

AMBASSADOR
Soi 11, Sukhumvit Road
Tel: 254-0444/99, 255-0444/99
A sprawling complex that offers one of the city's biggest array of Asian and European restaurants. *$$$*

BAIYOKE SUITE HOTEL
130 Rajprarob Road
Tel: 255-0330/41
Bangkok's tallest hotel is in the midst of its biggest market. Dine at the Sky Lounge for a superb view of the city. *$$$*

SOL TWIN TOWERS
88 New Rama VI Road
Tel: 216-9555
An international-class 700-room hotel with easy access to the city's tourist and commercial areas. *$$$*

CHINATOWN HOTEL
526 Yaowarat Road
Tel: 226-0033, 226-1267
Good accommodations in the very centre of Chinatown. Ideal for explorers of back alleys and hidden markets. *$$*

Hua Hin
ROYAL GARDEN VILLAGE
43/1 Phetkasem Road
Tel: (032) 520-250/1
Bangkok off: 476-0022
A cluster of bungalows on a long stretch of beach. It is some distance north of town but there is a shuttle bus. *$$$*

SOFITEL CENTRAL HUA HIN
1 Damnernkasem Road
Tel: (032) 512-021/2
Bangkok off: 233-0974
The old Railway Hotel has been refurbished and turned into a splendid hotel by the sea. *$$$*

Royal Garden Village

MELIA HUA HIN
33 Naresdamri Road
Tel: (032) 512879/41
Bangkok off: 271-0205
A 5-star luxury resort right on the wide, sandy beach. All 297 rooms and suites have stunning views of the sea. *$$$$*

Chiang Mai

CHIANG INN
100 Chang Klan Road
Tel: (053) 270-070/1
Bangkok off: 256-9112
A large hotel but a good base for explorations of Chiang Mai. *$$*

SURIWONGSE
110 Chang Klan Road
Tel: (053) 270-051
Bangkok off: 251-9883
One of the town's oldest hotels and adjacent to the Chang Klan night market. *$$*

RINCOME
301 Huay Kaew Road
Tel: (053) 221-130
Bangkok off: 252-6118
A low-rise hotel that offers a quiet ambience and good restaurants. *$$*

RIVER VIEW LODGE
25 Charoenprathet Road
Tel: (053) 271-109/10
A modest hotel with a lovely view overlooking the Ping River. Breakfast on the terrace is a great way to start the day. *$$*

Mae Hong Son
HOLIDAY INN MAE HONG SON
10/3 Khunlumpraphat Road
Tel: (053) 612-324/9
Bangkok off: 539-5156
Just south of town but with a spacious garden. Close to activities along the Pai River. *$$*

Northeast
Korat
CHOMSURANG
2701/2 Mahadthai Road
Tel: (044) 257-081/9
Comfortable city centre hotel. *$*

Ubon
PATUMRAT
173 Chayagkun Road
Tel: (045) 241-501/8
Bangkok off: 279-0486, 279-5463
Good downtown hotel. *$*

Phuket
Phuket Town
METROPOLE
1 Soi Surin, Montri Road
Tel: (076) 215-050
Bangkok off: 254-8197
Downtown and far from beaches but superb city accommodations. *$$$*

Patong
PATONG MERLIN
99/2 Moo 4 Patong Beach
Tel: (076) 340-037/8
Bangkok off: 253-2536
Low-rise holiday resort with easy access to the beach. *$$$*

CLUB ANDAMAN BEACH RESORT
77/1 Patong Thaviwong Road
Tel: 340-530
Bangkok off: 270-1627, 270-0957
A garden and spacious grounds with individual bungalows for guests. Real holiday living. *$$*

Bang Thao
SHERATON GRANDE LAGUNA BEACH
Bang Thao Beach
Tel: (076) 324-101 (7 lines)
A 5-star luxury beachfront resort on exclusive Bang Thao Bay. *$$$$*

DUSIT LAGUNA
390 Srisoontorn Road
Tel: (076) 324-320/32
A magnificent stretch of sandy beach and flanked by two inland lagoons, perfect for lazing in the sun. *$$$$$*

Nai Yang
PEARL VILLAGE RESORT
PO Box 93
Tel: (076) 327-006, 327-015
Enviable location on the beach at Nai Yang National Park. 177 rooms, coffeeshop, snack bar. *$$$$*

Kata

THE BOATHOUSE INN
Kata Beach
Tel: 330-557/60
Bangkok off: 254-5365
Luxury at the edge of the beach. Beautifully appointed rooms and one of the best restaurants on the island. Quiet corner of the beach. *$$$$*

Kata Noi

AMARI KATATHANI HOTEL
Kata Noi Beach
Tel: (076) 330-124/7
Bangkok off: 267-9708/10
The main hotel on a small, pine-shaded cove and one of the prettiest shorelines in Phuket. *$$$*

Karon Noi

LE MERIDIEN PHUKET
8/5 Mu 1, Tambon Karon
Amphoe Muang, P.O. Box 277
Tel: (076) 340-480/1
Bangkok office: 254-8147/8
Too large for some but self-contained and ideal for others. With its own private beach. *$$$$*

Nai Harn

PHUKET YACHT CLUB
23/3 Viset Road
Tel: 381-156/7; Bangkok off: 254-5335/6
Beautifully landscaped to hug a hill and on a lovely beach. A 5-star hotel. *$$$$$*

HEALTH & EMERGENCIES

Hygiene

Tap water is not safe to drink. Drink bottled water or soft drinks and use tap water only for bathing and brushing teeth. Most hotels and restaurants offer bottled water and clean ice. Shops sell plastic bottles of purified water.

Health Precautions

Stomach upsets are normally caused by over-indulgence. Most seafood is hygienically prepared but many foreigners overeat and their stomachs react negatively to a sudden switch of food.

Malaria has been reduced in the North, but the occasional case surfaces, usually in villages. If trekking, sleep under a mosquito net and apply mosquito repellent. Maloprim and other prophylactics are virtually useless. With its thriving nightlife and transient population, Bangkok is a magnet for sexually transmitted diseases. Take adequate precautions.

Pharmacies

Pharmaceutics are produced to international standards, and pharmacies must employ registered pharmacists. Most city pharmacists speak English.

Health Emergencies

First-class hotels have doctors on call to treat medical emergencies. For more serious cases, ambulance service is comparable to those in major Western cities, with Intensive Care Units equipped to handle any emergency. Many doctors have been trained in Western hospitals but the locally-trained doctors are equally good.

Hospitals

Bangkok: Samitivej Hospital at 133 Soi 49, Sukhumvit Road (Tel: 392-0011, 392-0061); Bamrungrat Hospital at 33 Soi 3, Sukhumvit Road (Tel: 253-0251/2); and the Bangkok Adventist Hospital at 430 Phitsanulok Road (Tel: 281-1422, 282-1100) are excellent.

Chiang Mai: Hospitals include Lanna Hospital, off the Superhighway northeast of town (Tel: 211-037), and Suan Dok Hospital, corner of Boonrungrit and Suthep Roads opposite Wat Suan Dok (Tel: 221-122).

Phuket: Go to Vajira Hospital, near the intersection of Yawaraj and Komara Pat Roads (Tel: 211-114); or the new Phuket International Hospital on Chalerm Phrakiat Road (Tel: 210-935/6).

Medical Clinics

Bangkok: There are many polyclinics, with specialists in several fields. The

British Dispensary at 109 Sukhumvit Road (between Sois 5 and 7, Tel: 252-8056) has two British doctors on its staff.

Chiang Mai: Numerous medical clinics treat minor ailments and are open until early evening. Two such clinics are: the International Emergency Centre (between Suriwong Book Centre and Thai Farmers Bank. Tel: 331-868), and the McCormick Clinic (Tel: 241-107, 241-311).

Phuket: There are several clinics along Soi Bangla on Patong Beach.

Police Emergencies

In **Bangkok**, the police emergency number is 191. There is also a Tourist Police unit formed specially to assist travellers (Tel: 195). Find them at the Tourist Assistance Centre at the Tourism Authority of Thailand (TAT) headquarters, and on the corner of Rama 4 and Silom roads. In **Chiang Mai** the tourist police can be reached at Tel: 248-974 and in **Phuket**, Tel: 212-213, 212-468. Most members of the force speak some English.

COMMUNICATIONS & NEWS

Most hotels have telephones, telegrams, mail, telex and FAX facilities. First-class hotel rooms have IDD phones; others have operators. To call abroad directly, first dial the international access code 001, followed by the country code: Australia (61); France (33); Germany (49); Italy (39); Japan (81); Netherlands (31); Spain (34); UK (44); US and Canada (1). If using a US credit phone card, dial the company's access number. Sprint, Tel: 001 999 13 877; AT&T, Tel: 0019 991 1111; MCI, Tel: 001 999 1 2001. Otherwise, make long distance calls in **Bangkok** at the General Post Office (GPO) annex, ground floor of the Nava Building on Soi Braisanee, just north of the GPO. Open 24 hours.

In **Chiang Mai**, the GPO on Charoenmuang Road (near the railway station) is open Monday–Friday, 8.30am–12pm, 1–4.30pm; Saturday, 9am–12pm. Services include letters, left messages, overseas telephone calls, and packing services. A handy branch office is Soi Braisanee, one block north of Tapae Road at the end of the Naowarat Bridge.

The **Phuket** GPO is at the intersection of Montri and Thalang roads. Open: Monday–Friday, 8.30am–12pm, 1–4.30pm; Saturday, 8.30am–12pm. Patong Post Office, on the beach road at Soi Patong Post Office, is open Monday–Friday, 8.40–12pm, 1–4.30pm; Saturday, 8.30am–12pm.

Newspapers

The *Bangkok Post* and *The Nation* are among the best and most comprehensive English-language dailies in Asia. The *International Herald Tribune* and *Asian Wall Street Journal* dailies as well as UK, French, German, and Italian newspapers are available at hotel newsstands.

USEFUL INFORMATION

Export Permits for Antiques

The Fine Arts Department prohibits the export of all Buddha images, images of other deities, and fragments (hands or heads) of images created before the 18th century. Shops can register other art objects for you. Otherwise, take it to the Fine Arts Department in Bangkok on Na Prathat Road together with two postcard-sized photos of it.

USEFUL ADDRESSES

Tourism Authority of Thailand

In **Bangkok**, the Tourism Authority of Thailand (TAT) office, at 372 Bamrungmuang Road, has brochures on accommodations, travel agents, car rental, and other services. Pleasant staff will answer your questions. Telephone TAT at 226-0060, 226-0072, 226-0085, 226-0098 (ext 311–317) for information. All TAT offices are open from 8.30am–4.30pm, Monday–Friday.

The **Chiang Mai** TAT office is at 105/1 Chiang Mai–Lamphun Road (Tel: 248-604, 248-607); the ground floor has an office of the Tourist Police.

In **Phuket**, the TAT is at 73–75 Phuket Road in Phuket town (Tel: 212-213, 211-036).

Index

ACKNOWLEDGMENTS

Cover	Steve Van Beek
Backcover	Hans Höfer
Photography	Steve Van Beek *and*
Pages 11	Hans Höfer
12B	Luca Invernizzi Tettoni
Cover Design	Klaus Geisler
Cartography	Berndtson & Berndtson
Copy Editor	Loh Ai Leen
Editorial Assitant	Luna Ho
Handwriting	V Barl

NOTES